MW00605976

The Charm of the Road

Drives in Jackson County

Jeanne Jorgensen

Glenn Oaks Publishing

i

The Charm of the Road
Drives in Jackson County, Iowa
Jeanne Jorgensen

Glenn Oaks Publishing
P. O. Box 672
Maquoketa, IA 52060 USA

Copyright © 1998 by Jeanne Jorgensen

Cover design: Chuck & Jeanne Jorgensen, Curt & Rebecca Tubbs Lichter
Cover painting: By Rose Frantzen, "Backroad, Jackson County", oil on canvas
Interior design: Rebecca Tubbs Lichter
Production: Curt Lichter and Rebecca Tubbs Lichter
Illustrations: Edd Scheer
Map design: Mark Anderson

This main text of this book was set in Garamond typeface.

All rights reserved. No part of this book may be reproduced or transmitted in any form or by any means, electronic or mechanical, including photocopying, recording, or by any information storage and retrieval system without written permission from the author, except for the inclusion of brief quotations in a review.

The purpose of this book is to entertain. The author and Glenn Oaks Publishing have tried to be as accurate as possible, but take no responsibility for any changes that have occurred since the printing of the book. The author and the publisher shall have neither responsibility or liability to any person or entity with respect to any loss or damage caused, or alleged to be caused, directly or indirectly, by the information contained in this book. If the purchaser of this book cannot accept these conditions, the book may be returned for a full refund.

Library of Congress Catalog Card #:   97-94448

ISBN: 0-9660709-0-9
10   9   8   7   6   5   4   3   2   1

First printing 1998

Printed and bound in the United States of America

ACKNOWLEDGEMENTS

Somewhere along the road to being, a book like this seems to take on a life of its own. The author begins by putting words on paper and soon the words grow into a book, and eventually, it seems taken over by a need to move out into the wide world. Other hands and minds become involved with its shaping and its growth. Like a child, it resembles its parents, but has a separate and unique personality. A finished book may be quite similar to the one the author envisioned, but it is also the product of all who helped along the way. Thus, a book reaches out and affects many lives even before it is published.

With those thoughts in mind, I would like to take this opportunity to thank those "other hands and minds" who helped shape this book.

Thank you to:

• *The Survey of Limestone Architecture of Jackson County*, prepared for the Jackson County Historical Preservation Commission, by Molly Myers Naumann, consultant, and many able county volunteers. This work inspired me to actively search out the limestone buildings and that search led to the study of old and new maps of the county. As I studied the maps, the doors of possibility were opened. I was captivated by the wealth of charm of Jackson County's historical and natural landscape.

• Karen Manning, and the Maquoketa Public Library staff for directing me to materials and ordering books on Inter-library Loan.

• Catherine Jorgensen Anderson, my daughter, for her many hours of computer guidance, to me, a complete novice.

• Mark Anderson, son-in-law, for expert work on the computer-generated maps and general computer suggestions galore.

• Bel Tubbs, and other volunteers at the Jackson County Historical Museum and Genealogy Library, who directed me to materials I would have never known about otherwise.

• Readers of the first draft: Bel Tubbs, Eleanor Busch and Barb Deutmeyer, who made suggestions on grammar and content. (Any mistakes are all mine.)

• To the neighbors and acquaintances who visited with me about the Jackson County they have known. Their snippets of memories are reflected in the Ghost Hamlets chapters. (The characters in the stories are, however, all fictitious and any resemblance to anyone, alive or dead, is purely coincidental.)

• Edd Scheer, for his willingness to adapt his artwork to suit my idea of "charm".

• Rose Frantzen, for graciously sharing her beautiful painting for the book's cover. The painting was an inspiration to me– months before I began the book– when I first saw it at her Old City Hall Gallery (121 South Olive Street, Maquoketa). All through the writing, the painting stayed in my mind's eye, inspiring and beckoning.

• Rebecca M. Tubbs Lichter, who did the time-consuming work of formatting the text, drawings and maps into a camera-ready copy for the printer. Her many late hours were a gift to the project that raised it to a truly professional level.

• Curt Lichter, who was enthusiastic about the book early on, and even up to its publication, and for his willing work on the printing phase of the book. His negotiating and knowledge allowed us, complete publishing novices, to publish a beautiful book. We can never thank him enough, for it is doubtful if there ever would have been a book, but for his guidance.

• Chuck Jorgensen, my husband, driver/pilot, poet and friend, who said, "Go ahead and write that book". And then said, "Let's start our own publishing company". We called it GLENN OAKS , after the Glen in each of our names, (Charles Glenn, and Glenith Jeanne) and the oaks on our beloved prairie and the land by the Mississippi. Chuck gives his all to any project he is working on, and his support and work made this book possible.

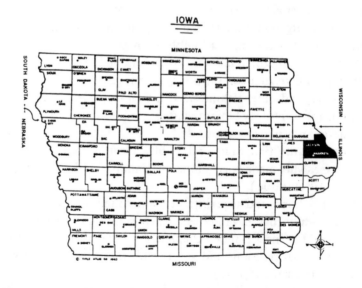

$\mathcal{C}$ontents

DEDICATION

To my daughters, Caytie and Meg, who were my first and most important creative project. Their lives enrich mine and I consider their friendship a mainstay. And to Chuck, my husband, who has always been a part of the creative side of my life, whether it be babies or books.

INTRODUCTION

> "Jackson County was named after Andrew Jackson the first
> president who had gone to Washington from the west. From
> Jackson came some radicalism, hatred of banks and of all
> precedents. The new Jacksonians were lovers of freedom, they
> were restive under restraint, and did not want a great deal of
> government over themselves, and above all, they wanted those
> who administered that government to be their servants."
>
> *History of the People of Iowa*
> Cyrenius Cole

The above quote might tell us something about the people who settled Jackson County and about their expectations. They came west for freedom of thought and freedom *from* governmental controls. Another aspect of choosing this place to live was the natural scenic beauty, attractive in each of the distinct landforms of the county. Those landforms range from the spectacular bluffs along the Mississippi, to the tiny, unique prairies scattered here and there, to the farm fields laid out on gently rolling hills with folds and dips, terraces and contour strips. There are very few places that lack a view; we are a farseeing land. Our motto here is "Jackson County, Simply Beautiful", and we have a lot to offer, for resident and visitor alike.

❖ For the urbanite, our land is like a theme park called
  "Jackson County: The Land of Farms and Parks".

❖ For the history buff, we might be an open air museum called
  "Jackson County: Land of the Black Hawk Purchase and the
  New American Frontier".

❖ For those who love *quaint*, we have it in this vast movie set;
  the movie might be titled: "In Old Jackson County", or
  "The Kilns of Jackson County".

❖ For the nature lover, we have a bountiful diversity in
  "Jackson County: Land of Hunting, Fishing, Camping, Hiking,
  Biking, Birdwatching, Spelunking and Wildflower Viewing".

Unlike a theme park that exists only for visitors, we also have a real life. Every day our communities are involved in farming, maintaining schools, providing health care, offering church activities, upgrading businesses, and all the other normal routines that keep the 20th century speeding towards the 21st. Even in the rush of busy lives, the genuine, "just folks" friendliness of our citizenry is one of the appeals of the area. Jackson County's charm is on the subtle side, and far from the glittering lights, hype and cuteness of a theme park, we are the real thing. That is why this book came to be. *It exists to encourage all who live here to experience the beautiful land in which we reside, as well as to tell the folks passing through about its special charms.*

I hope that you will see Jackson County with the eyes of an old friend, who stumbles onto the joy of a renewed acquaintance; or with the eyes of a new friend, who experiences the county with a sense of excitement and discovery.

HISTORICAL TIME LINE

8000 B.C.—
Formation of prairie after last glaciation.

200 B.C.-300 A.D.—
Woodland Indians inhabit area that will become known as Jackson County.

1673—
Marquette and Joliet, explorers, descend the Mississippi River and glimpse the shores of what will become Iowa.

1700-1800—
The Mesquakie and Sauk are pushed west by settlement in their homeland of Michigan and enter the lands along "The Father of Waters", the Mississippi River.

1788-1810—
Julien Dubuque's Lead Mines south of Dubuque. Miners explore south into Jackson County. (The Mesquakie, or Fox as the French called them, were partners with Dubuque in the mining business.)

[1600-1803]—
Mississippi Valley is in the hands of the Spanish, the French, the English, and finally the United States of America, who gains control with the Louisiana Purchase. At that time settlers began to trickle into the region.

1832—
Black Hawk Purchase: A strip of land, including Jackson County area, is opened to settlement.

1834—
Bellevue and Charleston (Sabula) get started.

1836—
Clark's Trail laid out by the Pence brothers.

1838—
Goodenow settles at the Forks of the Maquoketa. (Also known as Goodenow's Corners)

1839—
Bellevue War: A gun-battle on Riverview St. The questions remain: Was Brown a horse-thieving villain or an innocent victim; was Colonel Cox a hero or a bloodthirsty vigilante?

1843—

Iowa Band: News of the shoot-out reaches the Congregational Seminary back East, where eleven young men decide to come West and bring the Gospel to the lawless territory. Known as the Iowa Band, they establish Iowa College in Davenport- later moved and called Grinnell College. The Iowa Band was a contributing factor in the commitment Iowa has always had to excellence in education.

1846—

Iowa becomes a state. First governor is Ansel Briggs of Andrew.

1849-1850s—

California Gold Rush and westward expansion. Thousands of "movers" pass through Jackson County. Some settle, many watermills are built along the rivers and streams; first limestone houses built in county. Singing schools are the young people's entertainment. Dances are enjoyed by all ages.

1860s—

Civil War: Jackson County sends many men to fight. Women take over the operation of businesses and farms in their absence.

1870s—

Farm economy expands with the adequate railroad transportation for goods. Corn becomes a main crop and is fed to more hogs. The first commercial creamery is established in Iowa. Suffragette Movement gains momentum. Traveling troupes of actors entertain.

1880s—

Development of farm unions such as the Grange and the Populist Party. The railroad has caused a redistribution of village population. Mills are closing, and people moving to be near the trains. Town life sees the growth of community, service and social clubs. Artistic and cultural events are stressed as the way towns express their viability. Chatauqua entertains.

1890s-1916—

Stability is the norm. ("The Comfortable Years") More young women have goals of high school graduation, higher education and careers in business, nursing, education. The major industry in the county is Hurstville Lime Kilns. The "Big Woods" is cut down for cordwood to fuel the kilns. Farming is still the major way of life and the economic mainstay. Live performances at opera houses by vaudeville acts. Automobile replaces the horse and buggy. Aeroplanes overhead. "Moving Pictures"!

1917—

World War I changes everything. Our county's insulated and comfortable way of life is opened up to the world's problems and attractions.

1920s—

The economy booms, women cut their hair and also get the vote. Prohibition makes drinking and its lifestyle attractive to both young men *and* women. The Flapper Era. "Talkies"!

1930s—

The Great Depression, record drought and heat. Little cash money. Those living on farms, or those who can raise their own food, fare better in providing for their families. Industry and college vie for county young. Movies are the popular entertainment.

1940s—

World War II and once again the men of the area leave to fight the enemies of our way of life. Once again, women step in and take over farm work and factory jobs, and in the midst of anxiety and sadness over war losses, the county feels a sense of purpose and accomplishment.

1950s—

Industry expands. Many homes and farms are modernized. The draft horses of pre-war days are becoming rare. Television becomes a part of our entertainment.

1960s—

Modernization continues and many great old buildings, in town and on farms, are torn down or restructured. More land is put into farm production. More young people move away after high school graduation. More roads are paved. The Viet Nam Conflict calls the young away to war, and causes some friction in schools and on "Main Street". Community-based entertainment expands in the form of community theater, community chorus, sporting events and talent shows.

1970s—

Fuel shortages and harsh winters change the way our public buildings look. The windows are closed up with insulating material to save money, or buildings are torn down for newer structures. More industries come to the county.

1980s—

The approaching Sesquicentennial celebrations of several communities in Jackson County encourage more public awareness of our historical heritage. More emphasis on restoration of architecture and land preservation. Interest extends to archaeological survey of our prehistoric treasures.

1990s—

A period of prosperity is in place. Many homes are spruced up and some, over a century old, are painted and decorated in a historically correct fashion. Flower gardens spring up on farms, along highways and on quiet residential streets. Bellevue River Walk is built. Art galleries, gift shops, fine restaurants, camping and biking opportunities in the county draw more tourists. City and county pride is on the increase. Good standard of living.

Chapter *1*
The Land Seen From the Road

> *"A book of seasons, each of which should be written in its*
> *own season and out of doors, or in its own locality,*
> *wherever it may be."*
>
> Thoreau

To drive the backroads of Jackson County is to be drawn on — over another hill, around a gentle curve, through a dark forest, across an open plain as vast as the one Stonehenge is built upon. There are no castles, but there are country churches, and there are hamlets, or as we say, "wide spots in the road". We have stone sculpture in cemeteries; barns standing solid and lonely against the horizon, the last building left of a once prosperous farm. We have the wide Maquoketa River, muddy and slow as it joins the Mississippi near Green Island, and we have trout streams with crystalline water, and tiny brooks which trickle away from the springs hidden under fountaining grasses.

The world travels to see the Mississippi River Valley, and it is nowhere more spectacular than from the bluffs of Jackson County. To find our hidden treasure, just open your eyes and see the charm of the road. "Charm" implies an element of magic, something beyond rational control which attracts and fascinates. There is a storybook appeal to a path leading through the dark woods or up a steep bluff.

We are so busy. Do we allow ourselves to experience the allure of nature? In her book *The Land*, written in 1951, Jacquetta Hawkes says urban society is living in the "topmost attics of the mind". Modern people are content to receive information and instruction without experiencing for themselves the very basis of their beliefs. Living in the present culture, we cut ourselves off from nature and from the enrichment of previous times, both physically and in the depths of our minds, where the "images of experience have formed in darkness since the first stir of life in pre-Cambrian seas". Modern culture becomes so removed from the creative forces that "ugliness pours" from it. We drastically alter the land on which we live, making survival into a formula of science rather than a joyous art.

Once it would seem that people were concerned with the "quality of life as a whole". Hawkes gives the example of the celebration of the Twelve Days of Christmas. She feels that the revelry and ritual were understood to be more important than the work done on those twelve days could ever be. Think of shutting down the InterNet for twelve days to really experience some of the information already gathered on the computer but never actually tasted. Think of closing all the stores for a three-day festival to celebrate life.

We live by a "new fetish", and it is *The Standard of Living*. Hawkes says we overvalue material worth without relating it to the enjoyment of our lives. We are content to live in the midst of stink and dirt and pollution in order to feed The Standard of Living, and we give up so much in the doing of it.

"Surely it is time to recognize not a standard of living, but a standard of values, in which beauty, comeliness and possibility of solitude have a high place among human needs." Hawkes's words are even more relevant today, in 1997, than when she wrote them forty years ago.

Here in Jackson County we seem to be balancing the teeter-totter; our natural heritage on one end of the plank, and land use by farming and development on the other end of the plank. We are a prosperous farming county, perhaps not as prosperous as others within the state, but surely overwhelmingly successful by the standards of the world. We have a diverse natural scene and have worked to carve out many parks and public access parcels for our citizens. Of course, we have our share of timbers being bulldozed down, native knoll prairies being scraped off for the cheap gravel, roads being cut through centuries-old oak savannas. There is still, however, a sense of balanced harmony between field and forest, and along the roads less-traveled. It is very possible to look out over vast timbers, and "fruited plains", and get in touch with the substance and rhythm of the land. The land is not a separate and alien world removed from humankind's experience. It is integral to the shaping of our values as much today as in the past when 80% of America's population was involved in farming.

Turn off the four-lane highway and onto a county road, gravel or paved, cut your speed to 50 mph, or even better, 30 mph, and you will see the wildflowers, the birds, the unusual vines and shrubs, the views of a prosperous land balanced between responsibility and need, between appreciation and consumption. You will see the evidence of the commitment to that standard of values.

The Sunday afternoon drive was something of an institution in the America of the Eisenhower years. Families would pile into the Chevy, or the Ford, and drive around checking out their neighborhood, near and far. My family loved to go for rides. We marked the progress of the crops, who had planted what, the clarity of the water at the best fishing holes, the new paint jobs on barns and houses. Sometimes we'd see friends and stop right in the middle of the road to visit, car to car. Those were fun trips, and I have the feeling the memories are a legacy which has shaped me more than I realized until I began this book.

The drives suggested here certainly can be done on a Sunday afternoon, but they can also be a picnic getaway over a lunch hour, or an early morning homage to the rising sun, even a peaceful benediction to a long work day. Any day of the week or any hour of the day is right for the discovery and enjoyment of Jackson County's backroads.

The emphasis of the drives in the following pages is more on "seeing" and less on checking things out. Of course, for many, the lulling motion of the car is enough, but I encourage you to seek more.

To see the best these roads have to offer and to be charmed will require a commitment. A commitment to awareness and to the possibility of balance and harmony. Resist looking at the ugly, at scenes that jangle. (Your mind will record them anyway without your permission, storing it all away for future reference, if needed.) Keep your comments to what is uplifting, and you will be uplifted, too. Seek out interesting colors and shapes, look for the balanced or the pleasingly asymmetrical, think about our history and savor as much of the beautiful as you can find. In this way you will come to experience the charm of the road.

"Comments" imply someone to share these drives with. A navigator and pilot is the optimum crew, more than that and there gets to be too much "chitchat", which can distract from the view outside the car.

Someone to share a touch of extraordinary beauty with— that is a true blessing. I hope you all have a spouse or a friend who will occasionally be navigator to your pilot, then the drive becomes a truly fulfilling hour. If you go alone, listen to the other voices within yourself— the ones that don't do much talking out on the streets of home: the poet, the artist, and the philosopher. Listen and share with yourself; that's good, too. Each trip can be an adventure of pleasant aspect.

As you read this book, you will hear me refer to "we". My pilot and companion on all the drives has been my husband, Chuck, who has always encouraged the sharing of experiences. I thank him for his good-natured attitude, his words of encouragement, his sage comments on the book's contents, and his solid friendship.

And now I offer this blessing to all of you who take up the quest of seeking the charm of the road:

May the road rise to meet you
May the breeze be always at your back,
May the sun shine warm upon your face,
May the rain fall soft upon your fields,
And until we meet again
May you be held in the hollow of God's Hand.

Friendship

I know our friendship is a blessing
a flowering of the Holy Spirit between us
that you are a gift to me,
that what we feel has meaning deeper than we can imagine
that in a larger context we must bow
politely to one another in awe of this mystery

Let us then thank each other quietly as we meet and depart
let us remember to discuss our real lives
let us feel at ease allowing laughter and tears
to touch us in their own season
and let us keep moving together

For I also know there is nothing more than this joy of friendship
that separates us from the grave
and the warm presence of eternal night and repose
the joy of friendship being a scream of defiance
out a second story window after midnight
a noise that can reach up to the stars and rearrange
the very constellations that would dare tell us our future

Charles Jorgensen

Chapter *2*

Limestone Loops

> *no one saw, no one heard*
> *as an invisible God made rock*
> *in a wordless workshop*

from *Monuments*
Charles Jorgensen

OF LIMESTONE

People seem to have a special affinity for the rock which we use to construct our buildings. Perhaps it is the stability it provides, because we find ourselves turning back to it, judging our accomplishments by the magnitude of our stone buildings. The liberal rationalist, Professor G.M. Trevalyn writes of "the brotherly love we feel. . . for trees, flowers, even for grass, nay even for rocks and water". He speaks of "our brothers the rocks".

The Christian Church is founded on Peter, the Rock. Our gravestones, cut from granite and marble and limestone, are reminiscent of the monoliths of the pagans. Nevertheless, they are used in the Christian cemeteries more often than any other material.

Cut stone has been a part of civilization. In fact, it may be a definition of civilization, and the amount used is a gauge for the important center of a culture. Neolithic communities hauled megalithic blocks to their communal tombs, Bronze Age men built their temples of the sarsan stones, the Iron Age Celts gathered stones for tribal strongholds. The Romans used stone for both military sites and for their public buildings. The medieval peasants bathed cathedral stones with their sweat and dedicated their lives to working on the massive stone churches. The Tudor and Victorian periods in England saw the unprecedented use of tons of stone for public building, castles and garden ornamentations. When early settlers came to Jackson County, they built barns, houses, schools and churches out of the excellent, yellow limestone they found just below the surface of the land.

The builders had to have special knowledge to work in stone. All newly cut stone is permeated with quarry water which holds various minerals either dissolved or in suspension. On exposure, the quarry water is drawn gradually to the surface where it evaporates, depositing the minerals near the surface and so forming a tough outer skin. It is therefore more desirable that every block should first be cut into its final shape and then be allowed to season. That way it will go into the building with the skin unbroken. It is said that Christopher Wren, notable architect of St. Paul's Cathedral in London, would use no block unless it had been exposed for at least three years. The stone masons of our locale were knowledgable in the ways of stone. Their buildings stand as testament to their skill.

Every rural locality in Europe, especially in England and Germany, had its special products and skills, its peculiarities of agriculture, its own cuisine and customs. They looked around them for the materials with which to build their towns and a sense of harmony became a part of their buildings; they blended in with the landscape because they were built of the local materials. There seemed to be a beauty and rightness of the works of the generations who inherited the land.

When these folk left Europe, and came to America and then to Iowa, they brought the skill of working in local materials with them and some of our most satisfying architecture is reflective of their heritage. One has to wonder, if they had come in the 15th century, would we have whole villages of stone and flocks of sheep on the pastures?

What was the county like in 1850? To help us see with the eyes of the first dwellers we need firsthand accounts such as the following, part of an account by a mortality census taker, Wm. A. Maning:

> "The water is limestone - rock chiefly limestone. The soil is a dark loam with some sand. There is perhaps no county in the state possessing more advantages than this. It is well divided between timber and prairie land and is bountifully supplied with pure running waters. The fertility of the soil, the many valuable water privileges together with the fine timber and also iron ore that is found on the surface in lumps of a tons weight and the prospect of lead ore destines this county to be one of the best in the state. The timber adjacent to watercourses is principally oak, walnut, sugar tree, hackberry, elm and lime - on the uplands black and white oak, hickory and pin oak."

To comprehend the scope of the landscape and the character of the early villages, seems to me an important aspect of understanding the essence of our county. I very much suspect that the early settlers walked into a garden of rare beauty, but they could not appreciate it fully because they felt in competition with nature. They felt nature was to be conquered. It is my hope that we of the 20th century, and those of the 21st century, will learn how to grasp the significance of such beauty. I hope we will come to know how this living land can enhance our lives and share both its bounty and healing beauty with us.

9

Monuments

For millions of years,
shells fell through the depths
fragments of bones and mud cemented
by a tightening fist through eternal night
no one saw
no one heard
as an invisible God made rock
in a wordless workshop

Then the water slid
off the back of the continent
eventually
the endless fields of labor
exposed to human hands
to blast it, haul it,
work it for our own foundations
drive on it or simply throw it just for fun
in spasms
of youthful folly

Occasionally, we look at it
appealingly common
smelling of the dust of time
its endless colors leading us to tangled dreams
of a woman's golden hair
or of the gown of a Goddess
rippling before our eyes

If we could open an inner eye
as we drive by those walls of stone
we would know

here stands a house
built before time existed
lifted out and honored
by callused hands and all too human hearts
monuments
to the moments of creation

Charles Jorgensen

10

The St. Donatus Drive

There were a few days each summer in San Francisco, 1968-70, that we called "Iowa days". The clouds were white and popcorn puffy and although the breeze was cool, the sun shone warmly. The fresh-cut grass smelled a little like an Iowa town on a Saturday afternoon. On those days I daydreamed about my home state. I dreamed about green grass and sparkling cornfields, limestone houses and red barns. Then I'd study the map of Iowa, looking for the perfect little town to move to when our Navy stint was over. I often noticed the town of St. Donatus and wondered about "the picturesque French village", as the map then called it.

Jackson County had so many little towns with interesting names: Baldwin (a family name), Sabula, Zwingle. The North Fork of the Maquoketa River and Tete Des Morts Creek were names that promised special beauty and a kind of rugged romance.

So when we moved back home we began to search out these places. Luck or some other form of chance, perhaps grace, brought us to Maquoketa to live. Now nearly thirty years later, those daydreams have come true and are just "down the road".

St. Donatus is a treasure chest full of limestone structures made not by the French, but by immigrants from Luxembourg, a country touched by France on one side and Germany on the other. The texts carved on the gravestones in both the Catholic and Lutheran cemeteries are in German. A woman is referred to as "Frau" and a man's name is preceded by "Herr". When that former map of Iowa came out with its words, "French village", it must have caused a few snorts of derision in St. Donatus among the people of Luxembourg descent.

Along this tour you will see the broad valleys which drain the high farmland plateau to the west. Here the gravel roads seem to keep the valley streams company, running along beside them on their trips down to the Mississippi. Many of the streams are springfed, their little chuckling brooks trickle along to meet larger streams in the deep valleys.

The valleys are forested with oak trees, and seem like parks; open and shady lawns. There are groves of hickory and walnut as well, and the mulberry trees droop heavy-laden with fruit in July— the berries fall on the roadway staining the rocks and dust purple.

The fallow pastures flanking the road have vast bouquets of blooms that some call weeds! But a few of these plants were at home on the prairie, the little dry upland prairies that could survive on the rocky knolls and were abundant when the settlers came into the valleys.

Many of the flowering weeds are invaders, coming to the New World on the ships of the earliest settlers. Nevertheless, they serve a helpful role in the ecology of the pasture, providing nectar for bees and butterflies and their root systems give

11

stability to the hillsides. They are richly colorful, their combinations make a pleasing pastel palette.

One bluffside pasture in late July had over ten kinds of blossoms ranged up its side. The list included plants of low, middle and tall heights. Close to the ground and at the front of the view, were purple vetch, pink clover, and yellow birdsfoot trefoil. Then, in the middle range were fluffy, lavender bergamot mixed in with field daisies, and tiny, white daisy fleabane. The tallest flowers were in the back: sturdy golden black-eyed Susans next to delicate, white Queen Anne's lace; jewelweed, pale yellow blossoms dancing in the breeze beside hawkweed, bright yellow heads standing to attention above the rest. It was as though a landscape gardener had arranged them by height and temperament. Small orange butterflies were busy in the flowers, and the air was buzzing with the sound of bumblebees at work. Overhead, bluish white clouds raced before a brisk wind.

On Sieverding Ridge, 320th Street, and then Centerville Road, D53, the way opens up on the high top of the land with spectacular views all around. The cornfields are like a sparkling blue-green counterpane spread across the hills. Today in mid-July, there is a hint of emerging brown tassels and the fields look like they have a crew haircut, with the hundreds of short, brown spikes poking above the green plain. The soybean fields look like crushed-velvet cushions of bright green laid down in rows across the gently swelling hilltops. Nearer to St. Donatus are strip fields, with contour terraces draped over the hills like necklaces; bronze of ripe oats and amber of buckwheat.

This area has many dairy farms taking advantage of the lush grasses rich with limestone nutrients. The black and white Holsteins possess the steep pastures and are peaceful and sturdy against the deep green grass. The occasional flock of sheep lend the hills a very "Old World" look.

Tour St. Donatus, the village, with the guidebook, "Historic Sites in Jackson County, Iowa", and "Luxembourg In America", available at the Jackson County Welcome Center at Sabula or at the Chamber of Commerce Offices in Maquoketa or Bellevue, or get a map from Kalmes Store in St. Donatus. While there, get the makings of a picnic lunch: cheese, sausage, fresh fruit and juice or imported beer. Take these in a paper sack to the bench above the valley at the Lutheran Church; or back to the little shrine, Fritz Chapel on 308th Street; or find your own special spot to view the glorious scenery.

Beyond St. Donatus, and farther along on this stretch of High Bridge Road, a bridge crosses over a swift little stream; the map tells us it is the Tete Des Morts, a celebrated name. Local legend, and one of many versions of the story, has it first named in the 1600s by Father Hennipen, an early explorer and missionary. He came upon the remains of a great Indian battle at the foot of a bluff along the stream. (Not far from this bridge.) Tete Des Morts means "Heads of Death", and it brings to mind a grizzly picture of what Fr. Hennipen found there— a pile of skulls. The Italian explorer, Giacomo C. Beltrami, in his diary of the 1826 expedition up the Mississippi says, "...we saw a place called Death Heads, a field of battle where Foxes defeated the Kaskasias, whose heads they fixed on poles as trophies of their victory."

These little valleys draining the upper Mississippi were much favored by the Indians of historic as well as prehistoric times. Since around 1750 the Sauk and Fox (Mesquakie) Indians of northern Illinois and western Wisconsin used the land west of the Mississippi as hunting ground and to plant summer corn crops. In winter small bands of hunters with their family members would walk across the frozen river to hunt or to tap maple trees to make syrup. The native peoples lived in harmony with the bluffs and the streams and were at home all along the river.

> "Here our village [Rock Island] had stood for more than one hundred years, during all which time we were the undisputed possessors of the valley of the Mississippi, from the Ouisconsin to the Portage Des Sioux, near the mouth of the Missouri, being seven hundred miles in length."
>
> *Life of Black Hawk*
> Black Hawk

The Indians didn't dwell in Jackson County in large numbers at the time of European settlement. In the 1830s they were passing through, hunting and stopping at the log cabins of whites for food, but their villages had gone. In a short time even that yearly migration dwindled to a trickle of small family groups going back to their ancestral home across the Mississippi.

The bits of ancient pottery and the stone flakes we find along streams and newly plowed fields tell us of the prehistoric culture. The forests and prairie they knew have become farmlands. The abundance of a highly diverse landscape has now shifted to the high productivity associated with agribusiness; the hybridized crops and only a few types of animals present a landscape which lacks the diversity that was so evident before European settlement.

A trip to Europe leaves a lasting impression. I will always relive in my mind England in June: the intense, late afternoon sunlight streaming across Stonehenge; the unbelievably soft rain falling on the trout stream which runs through Lower Slaughter in the Cotswolds. The feelings of those places can be called up in memory and savored at will. The smells, sounds, the quality of light and the historical and natural sights are so unique that their essence stays powerfully alive in memory.

It was an unexpected delight to find the scenes of this place in Iowa, this little corner near the Mississippi's bluffs, coming back with clarity and with that hint of charm that usually accompanies the special and rare. This place is only twenty-five miles from my home! But it is true, the quaint and old stone buildings, the ordered and lush fields of corn and soybeans, the July sun shining down on the valleys, all made an experience as lasting in memory as one of those days in England. This fulfilled the expectations of 30 years ago - it was truly an "Iowa day".

"Many a tourist comes home to a land like this, weary and penniless, like Sir Launfal after his fruitless quest, to discover that the grail of health and rest and beauty which he sought afar so strenuously is most easily and readily found at home."

Some Summer Days in Iowa
Frederick Lazell, 1909

St. Donatus Loop Driving Description

(Note: In general, the "Avenue" roads run north and south; the "Street"roads run east and west. Suggestion: Carry a compass in the car for those overcast days when it is hard to find "north".)

This loop has houses which exemplify the Luxembourg influence on the area's architecture:

> "The limestone architecture of Jackson County is vernacular in form as well as material. Local crafts-men constructed houses and buildings in the simple, functional forms familiar to them."
>
> *Survey of Limestone Architecture of Jackson County,* 1990

This Luxembourgian style has primary facades on the eaves side, jerkin head roof is common; doors and windows are symmetrical, and the application of stucco is a very common element.

❖**From Bellevue take Highway 52 north to 308 St., turn west onto this gravel road.**
(1) Abandoned farmhouse circa 1846. It sits behind newer house. There was a log cabin in the farm yard a few years ago. Is it still there?
(2) St. Nikolaus Church and graveyard c. 1860. German Catholic congregation with ties to St. Donatus.
(3) Niemann House, painted white; c. 1845. It is considered to be the first stone house built in Jackson County. NRHP
(4) Fritz Chapel, a small stone structure with gable roof, built by Matthias Fritz to commemorate the safe voyage to America. c. 1852. Fritz handcarved the arches from a single piece of walnut, and also carved the Christ figurine.

❖**Turn right on Sieverding Ridge.**
(5) School on right, it even has a standing outhouse; becoming more and more rare.

❖**At 320 St., or D55, turn left. Continue to 258th Ave., and turn north.**
(6) Abandoned farmhouse, little out building and barn are also of interest.

❖**At D53 turn right.**
(7) A gable roof house, stuccoed. 1860

❖**Continue to St. Donatus.**
Tour the city using the "Historic Sites in Jackson County, Iowa," guidebook which is available at the Jackson County Welcome Center at Sabula, or the Chamber Offices in Bellevue or Maquoketa, or in St. Donatus, at Kalmes Store. Be sure to go into the Gehlen House, one of the earliest limestone buildings in the county.

❖**Proceed east on D53 which becomes High Bridge Road east of St. Donatus.**
(8) Stuccoed house, painted green, sits close to road. 1860
(9) A ruin behind a newer house, up a quarter-mile long lane.

❖**Turn south onto 346 Ave., and then right onto 370 St.**
(10) Ruin seen over the field to the north, surrounded by brush and trees.

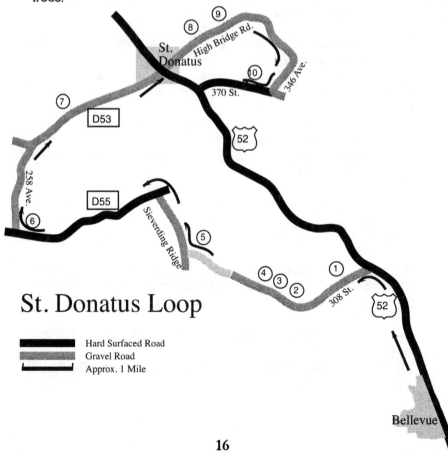

St. Donatus Loop

▬▬▬ Hard Surfaced Road
▬▬▬ Gravel Road
┗▬▬▬┛ Approx. 1 Mile

Bellevue Township Loop

Impressive limestone buildings and spectacular scenery are the highpoints of this loop. The roadside flowers, in every blooming season, can be seen in ditches, pastures and timbers. Along Big Mill trout stream in July we saw tickweed, or Black-eyed Susan, and Joe Pyeweed. There are bluebird houses on many fenceposts.

Continuing up the valley, the road passes a marshy area fringed with cattails and alive with busy, swooping swallows. Then the road begins to climb up between steep pastures and large limestone chunks and outcroppings are everywhere. It looks dry here, giving it the feeling of the foothills of a mountain range out West. There are remnants of *oak savanna*. (See GLOSSARY for definition.) Suddenly, the road levels off on the flat upland and is surrounded by fields of corn and soybeans.

The 'B' level roads on this drive are distinct from each other: 289th Avenue is open, with scrub trees growing along the fencerows; but 258th Avenue becomes secluded as it passes through a woodland. It passes rocks covered with moss and ferns, more than are seen along most roads. Everything is shaded under a high canopy of tree branches. It is still and feels cool here in this shady lane. Here and there a shaft of bright sunlight strikes down on green, translucent ferns and velvety moss. A glade opens up briefly in a remnant of oak savanna looking like a royal hunting park in Merry Old England. One thinks the royal deer may be just behind that copse of trees up the bluff. The ditches are fluffy with lavender beebalm and white Queen Anne's lace; bouquets for thousands. The butterflies flit in the sunshine from one bouquet to another, then cross the road in a slow, skipping flight.

Down the long valley of Mill Creek is Paradise Valley. It was named by E.G. Potter when he chose this spot to settle in 1838. He had walked from St. Louis, Missouri, looking for land that fulfilled his concept of perfection. When he saw this valley it was like a paradise after the "purgatory" of his long trek north, as he later referred to it. Try to see the valley through his eyes and imagine what it must have looked like then, untouched by civilization and progress.

17

Bellevue Township Loop Driving Description

This Loop shows houses of German influence. Many have a hip roof, or a gable roof. They are square and are often covered by stucco. Many German stonemasons lived around Bellevue according to the 1870 Census.

❖**From downtown Bellevue head south on Highway 52 for about a half mile to Z15, or 362 St., proceed another half mile.**
(1) George Dyas House. The original Dyas settler had five sons and he built five houses for their families; several of brick, and several of limestone (one is partially demolished farther west on Z15). This house is of Gothic Revival influence. NRHP 1850s

❖**Turn around on 407 Ave. and come back on Z15 several hundred yards. Turn off on 243 St. Proceed slowly as there are children and animals crossing this road.**
(2) Kieffer Barn is to the north off the short 243 St. The building is well-maintained by the present owner who feels it may have originally housed the family, along with the livestock, while a house was being built.

❖**At Highway 52 turn left, heading north and back to Bellevue. In town turn left onto Highway 62 and leave town. At the west edge, just beyond Big Mill Creek Bridge, turn off to the right onto D61, the Bellevue-Cascade Road, which is paved.**
(3) 2 1/2 story gable roof house with additions. Stucco, c.1860-70
(4) Springhouse or cave entrance (difficult to see from the road.)

❖**At 216 St. turn off. This road climbs up out of the valley.**
(5) 2 story house at the intersection of D61 and 216 St.
(6) 1 1/2 story house. C.1850-60
(7) 2 story house, altered. 1860

❖**Turn onto 289 Ave., a Low-Maintenance Road, or 'B' level road. (Don't continue if conditions are muddy, or otherwise unsafe for driving.) At Bellevue-Cascade Road turn left and head west for a quarter mile or less and turn right onto 283 Ave. At 258 St., turn right and come back down the valley to the east.**
The middle portion of this road is shown as a 'B' level road, but it is well-maintained. This road joins Mill Creek Road, or D57, and takes you back into Bellevue to the east.

18

(8) 3 story house. Set back against the bluff, and seen across the stream and meadow. Stone sills and lintels, stucco scored to look like ashlar blocks. C.1850-60

(9) Big Mill Homestead, historic site maintained by Jackson County. The house was built by E.G.Potter and recently received a restoration grant, with work done on tuckpointing by a class in limestone wall repair through Clinton Community College, project funded by REAP. C.1850 NHRP Suggestion: Get out of your car and walk around it. It's a beauty.

(10) Paradise Farm includes two houses: one the original family home which houses the first lending library in Iowa; and a dormitory, built for the farmhands and visitors, which has been converted into a family dwelling. The dairy barn has recently been removed, leaving only one of its stone walls. All were built by E.G.Potter in 1846, and are currently not open to the public.

(11) 2 story hip roof house, stucco covered and scored to look like ashlar. It was built as a school for the Potter children. c.1850-60

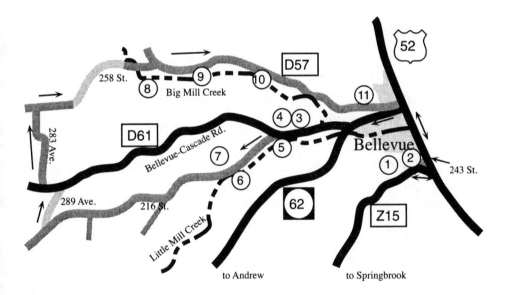

Bellevue Township Loop

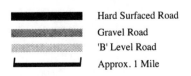

Hard Surfaced Road
Gravel Road
'B' Level Road
Approx. 1 Mile

19

Andrew Loop

The town of Andrew, first called Silsbee, was platted in 1841. It was a center of life in Jackson County for some time, being the County Seat and an important stop on the stage line from Davenport to Dubuque in the early years. It was the home of Ansel Briggs, who was a stagecoach operator and real estate developer before going to Iowa City in 1846 as the brand new state's first governor.

Rev. Wm. Salter, of the 1843 missionary "Iowa Band", mentions holding many church services in Andrew, where he made the acquaintance of Ansel Briggs. He preached here in December of 1843 in the upper story of the log courthouse.

The tour begins at Salem Lutheran Church. If you are lucky enough to find the doors open, slip in and sit on a wooden carved pew and feast your eyes on the perfectly proportioned baroque altar, highly carved, and painted white with gilt highlights. Plan your drive for a Sunday morning and attend worship services here if possible.

The Old County Jail is open during the summer, but if not, you can still see the metal cage-cell out in back of the building and visit the adjoining park to play on the playground equipment or have a picnic.

The country portion of the Andrew Loop might be called "the yellow coneflower drive", as it seems every ditch is blooming with these prairie flowers on this bright morning in late July. The drive also crosses two streams: Brush Creek, a trout stream to the east of Andrew; and Farmer's Creek to the west. At Brush Creek there is a small parking area just off 261st Avenue and a stile to help anglers get over the barbed wire fence for access to the stream. Cattle are pastured here; be cautious and also respectful of the farmer's property.

The stretch on 261st Avenue, after the iron bridge crossing Brush Creek is heavily timbered, dotted with large chunks of limestone covered with moss, ferns and wildflowers growing from the crevices of the stone. The woodland floor is deep with leaf mold and carpeted with the foliage of wild ginger.

The road then lifts up onto a high ridge. There is a frame house on 261st Avenue which I call "the sunrise/sunset house" because it would be a wonderful place to live to watch the sun rise and to watch it set every day. There is a long, clear view to both east and west.

Across Highway 62 on 189th and 184th Street are open pastures of savanna with contoured strip fields and timbers far into the distance. The church steeple at La Motte can be glimpsed to the northwest and off to the south is the Andrew watertower. There are several farm ponds along this route, shining amongst the trees and tall grasses. We saw a red cow and her nursing calf knee-deep in thick green grass by just such a pond, its surface reflecting the intense blue of the sky.

The country houses here have a character which is distinct from the other limestone houses in Jackson County. The double chimneys, the more reddish color of the stone, and the side lights are touches which make them very special among the special. A drawback for our viewing is that the houses are often set back at the end of a long lane and hard to see up close. But if you drive slowly past the DeFries farm, you will see a lovely example of this area's stone houses. Feast your eyes on the buildings beautifully maintained and set off by green lawns. There is a *hausspruch*, or datestone, in the center of the front wall over the door, written in German. Translated, it reads, "The best that we have, is God and His blessings."

Andrew Loop Driving Description

❖**In Andrew proceed to the corner of E.Emmet and N.Willough St.**
(1) This is the Salem Lutheran Church. It is often open to the public and has a carved wooden altar that is reminiscent of German Baroque. c.1875

❖**On to the corner of E.Emmet and N.Main**
(2) The old Jackson County Jail. The 3 story structure once served as the county jail (1871-1896), the city jail and a women's lockup during its heyday. An added treasure is the display of old drawings and etchings made by prisoners; these were discovered under layers of whitewash during restoration. For information on tours call 1-800-342-1837 at the Jackson County Welcome Center. NRHP c.1871

❖**From Andrew proceed north on Highway 62.**
(3) Nathaniel Butterworth House, a 2 1/2 story gable with side lights on either side of the entrance door, classical trim and paired chimneys. This was an inn and is a great example of 1850 limestone architecture. NHRP 1852

❖**Turn right on 154 St.**
(4) 2 story gable roof single end chimney. c.1860

❖**At 261 Ave., turn left (northeast), cross Brush Creek, to join 298 Ave. Continuing northeast. Once again join Highway 62 and drive west for about a third of a mile to 189 St. Cross Brush Creek again. Now turn off onto 184 St.**
(5) The Kilburg House, 2 story gable, entry with side lights, paired chimneys. 1850s. (A newer farm building obscures a close-up view from the road, wait to see it from across the valley at the Building for the Insane, Y61, or at the driveway to the County Cemetery off the 'B' level road, 184 St.)

❖**Turn right and join Y61; drive north.**
(6) Insane Asylum, or Building for the Insane. A 2 story gable, with iron grating still in place on some windows. A large wooden sign says, ANDREW JACKSON DEMONSTRATION FARM. 1870-72

❖**At 216 St. Turn left.**
(7) 2 story gable roof house, with shallow T wing, fenestration (window treatment) is unusual. 1860

❖**Continue on to 216 Ave. and turn left, south. (The road angles west.)**

(8) 2 story gable roof house.

❖**Turn off at 180 St., it will join with 232 Ave.**

(9) DeFries Farmstead. 2 story gable roof house with *hausspruch*, (year or inscription on carved stone at gable end), side lights, double end chimneys. NRHP 1850s. Also a 1 1/2 story gable roof building called a carpenter shop and a barn. NRHP 1850s.

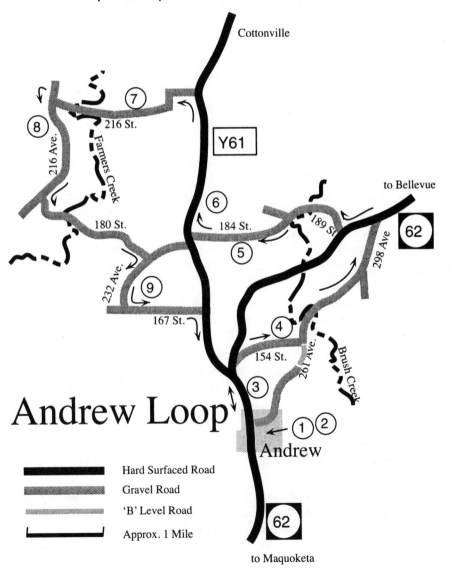

Clark's Trail Loop

This part of the county was first settled by white men in 1836 when the Pence brothers, Wallace and Solomon, were hired by a man named Clark to survey a road and ascertain possible fords on the Wapsipinicon and Maquoketa rivers. Clark had high hopes for the town of Buffalo, just south of Davenport, and wanted roads established in every direction to lure trade.

The Pence brothers worked out the trail that is now roughly our route on Y34. It came to be known as Clark's Trail or the Buffalo Road.

By the 1860s and 70s the little towns which had sprung up along Clark's Trail were prospering. On this loop are buildings, like the schools and houses, which reflect the abundance of prime limestone construction materials as well as the knowledge brought to the area by the German heritage settlers from Pennsylvania who had skills in stone construction.

Four of the stone buildings are schools; three of them are in very good condition. Several of the homes have been lived in for generations by the same family and are well-maintained.

The sites along this loop are spread out but set down amidst spectacular scenery, varying from rolling prospects to bluffed river valleys.

This blend of wild beauty and early settlement gives the drive a feeling of timelessness. If the towns along Clark's Trail had prospered, what would have become of these river valleys? Their appeal lies in their silent inaccessibility. They are havens for birds and wildflowers, for the deer and the red-tailed hawk. And they can also be havens for our image of the early days along the Buffalo Road.

We drove this loop in February of 1997, when an early spate of warm days had created high river levels. The water had just begun to recede and leave cakes of ice—some as large as a car, which the river had thrown up to litter the fields along its banks. The night before, when the flood waters were highest, the temperature had dropped and frozen a thin pane of ice around tree trunks and through bushes. When the flood waters receded the ice remained, some in a level sheet frozen to many twigs sticking up through it, and some breaking down and slanting from limbs and dried cornstalk rubble angled to the ground. When the sun's beams hit these ice fields, it was a dazzling spectacle. The ice acted as a thousand prisms and reflected every shade and hue in the color spectrum. We were struck with the raw power of the flood on the one hand, and on the other, the delicate beauty of the glass-like panes of the ice.

To experience such unplanned splendor was a moment of epiphany, to grasp, for a second, the manifestation of nature's character— such power tempered with a rare and fragile beauty. It was a scene we felt privileged to witness.

Clark's Trail Driving Description

❖**Begin at Mill Rock on 53 Ave. South of Baldwin.**
(1) Mill Rock School, recently refurbished by the County Conservation Board. c. 1869

❖**Continue north on Y34 through Baldwin. At 67 St. Turn west.**
(2) Tabor Farmhouse and Smoke House. The local lore says in pre-settlers time, Indians came to a spot in the front yard to hold tribal gatherings. They had a spectacular view over the rolling country and the sunrise. 1860

❖**Drive north on 32 Ave., then west on 83 St. and the stretch of 10 Ave. which leads to 30 Ave. Proceed and cross the South Fork of the Maquoketa River at the Millertown Access.**
(3) The limestone building in Section 28 has been altered and a new cedar addition added. This house, on the right, is up on a ridge after we have come through miles of river and creek valleys. It must have a wonderful view of sunsets.

❖**When 30 Ave. Meets E17, turn left, or west, and cross the South Fork once more and enter Canton.**
(4) Canton School, in Canton and near the river is in very good condition. It has rounded eyebrow window tops and carved wooden bargeboard under the eaves, and is crowned with a white belltower. NRHP 1877
(5) While in Canton look at the remaining foundation of Kelsall's Stone Store, to the northwest of the school on the second street south of E17. You will see the square blocks of stone and the gothic, or pointed, arch of the wooden door frame which led to the lower level. c. 1860-70.

❖**Backtrack on E17 to 6 Ave. And then left, or north. At 166 St., turn right, east, and proceed past 21 Ave.**
(6) Oak Grove School, the building's side wall has been breached to make a place to store hay. 1871

❖**Turn onto 45 Ave.**
(7) Central School, also known as Hickory Grove, is privately owned and maintained. The school is located at the intersection of the Bellevue-Canton and Dubuque-Canton roads. It was used until 1965. NRHP 1868 (Look to the east before proceeding for a glimpse of a limestone farmhouse nestled in among the trees.)

❖**Stay on a southerly course and eventually rejoin E17, left turn, for a half mile. Turn off on Y34 south.**
(8) Henry Lubben Farm. A 2 1/2 story farmhouse with gable roof. There are two stone outbuildings closeby. The stone was quarried a quarter mile west of the house. The walls are two feet thick. The spring house is built over a spring which only ran dry two times in the hundred years between 1858 and 1958. The smokehouse held the carcasses of twenty hogs at butchering. The cured "sides" were hauled to Davenport during the cold weather to be sold. NRHP 1858-60

❖**Still on Y34 and about a half mile south look to the east for**
(9) Sieben House. This house cannot be seen from the public road. It is a 2 1/2 story gable roof house and has two datestones or "*hausspruch*". Return to Baldwin.

Clark's
Trail
Loop

Hard Surfaced Road
Gravel Road
Approx. 1 Mile

The Maquoketa Township Drive

This drive takes us through town and then out to the north and east along the Maquoketa River, which is now at its full strength of combined North and South Forks. There are remnants of short grass prairie near here and the appeal of the river's valley is evident. If one can shut out the modern improvements of the last one hundred and fifty years, it is possible to see what attracted the settlers to this place back in 1838: rolling plains, the trees, the river and many streams. It was a place with the possibilities of plenty and it was appealingly beautiful.

Maquoketa, "the land of steady habits" near the forks of the Maquoketa River is beautifully situated on a fine rolling prairie and surrounded by the finest agricultural part of our county.

Wm. A. Maning, census taker, 1850

Stone buildings, with their unique atmosphere, have to be experienced to be understood. The sounds, both outside and inside, affect the ear more subtly, and the walls seem to provide more shelter. How lucky we are to have such lovely examples all around us here in Maquoketa and Jackson County. Costello's Old Mill Gallery is a perfect place to visit and find out for oneself all about being in a limestone house built nearly a century and a half ago.

Maquoketa Township Loop Driving Description

❖**From the intersection of Platt and Main, proceed west on West Platt, Highway 64, to S. Vermont, turn off to the left and go to 116 S. Vermont.**
(1) Basnett-Nickerson house, a 2 story hip roof, Italianate sans brackets. A fine restoration job evident. NRHP c.1870-75

❖**Return to W. Platt and drive east (on Highway 64) on E. Platt to the Fair Grounds corner; Highway 62 turns off to the left. Continue east on 62, crossing the Maquoketa River, to the hamlet of Bridgeport.** The school is on the hill to the left.
(2) Maquoketa Township School, called the Bridgeport School. More recent school children would know it as the Stange School where they might have spent "Old Country School Day" on a field trip. Stucco, c.1870

27

❖**Turn around at Dark Hollow Road and drive back toward Maquoketa on Highway 62. At Codfish Hollow Road, beyond the bridge, turn off to the right.** Along this road, 35 St., watch for prairie plants in the pastures and ditches. Continue to the house on the right side of the road; it sits back from its double avenue of trees. **(3)** Two story gable roof house. 1860 (It is said that the log house of Colonel Thomas Cox, early territorial legislator and surveyor of Jackson County, must have been near here on the north bank. Early records say his home, called Richland, was near the spot where the stagecoach road from Davenport to Dubuque crossed a rocky ford of the Maquoketa River.) This limestone house may have been close to the stage road.

❖**Turn at 281 Ave. and come back on Codfish Hollow Road to 233 Ave., called Seven Hills Road. Turn left, south, for a short cut to Highway 64.** On the left of 233 St., is a little stone building, down in its own little valley.
(4) A 1 1/2 story house with gable roof. c.1860

❖**Turn right onto Highway 64 and continue to Costello's Old Mill on your left.** Turn into their driveway and park in the lot by the old wagon and the gallery sign. Here is a chance to go into a limestone building and experience its very special qualities. The gallery is a super place to spend several enjoyable hours.
(5) Seneca Williams Mill, also known as The Oakland Mill. A 3 story gable roof. A new wooden millwheel has been added to the outside of the lower level on this lovingly restored building. NRHP 1868

❖While in Maquoketa, be sure to visit the Historic District on **West Pleasant St**. This street has some of the grand old houses of the last century. They are well-preserved with loving appreciation of their historic character. At the corner of W. Pleasant and S. Prospect is Squier's Manor, Maquoketa's own very special bed and breakfast.

Maquoketa Township Loop

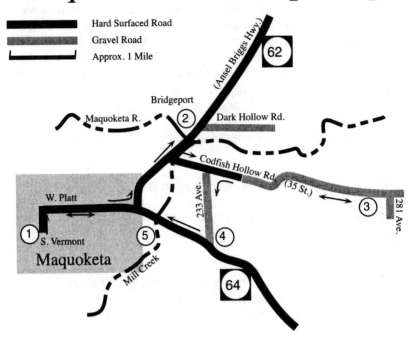

Hard Surfaced Road
Gravel Road
Approx. 1 Mile

The South Fork Loop

This drive takes us past superb examples of the works of the stonemasons. The houses look staid and rooted to the bit of earth they have claimed, and yet there is usually a touch of elegance to be seen, in a gothic window, or a bay window. One has been described as a "wonderful example of limestone architecture." The Hurstville Limekilns are certainly unique and because of their massive size are *certainly* impressive. They stand in their silent sentinel lineup evoking timeless images of stone towers and ramparts of the medieval past.

Try to shut out the cars and trucks, the pole buildings you will see along the drive, the water towers—the things of this century—and look for the lay of the land. In your mind's eye see the prairie's tall grasses and little streams running through them. There is a scarcity of trees in the southern part of the loop because in pre-settlement days it was a vast prairie. The once-dense forest that stood for miles around the Kilns is greatly diminished. As you look down on Maquoketa from either vantage, imagine its sand hills; its forested bluffs; its treeless plains of waving grasses, and the river dividing the two types of terrain. It might be possible for you to see the land as the first settlers saw it and to catch their excitement over its possibilities.

29

The South Fork Township Driving Description

❖**Driving west on Highway 64 in Maquoketa, turn left onto Western Ave., continue to W. Summit St. Turn right onto W. Summit and take the overpass which now becomes 33rd St. Go to the first intersection and turn left onto Myatt Drive, 184 Ave. This takes you in a southerly direction.** At 19 St., on the left, is the Anson Wilson House which from its hill, looks out over the surrounding fields, and the houses and trees of Maquoketa.
(1) Anson Wilson House, 2 story gable roof house and springhouse. It has been called "a wonderful example of limestone architecture". NRHP 1863

❖**Go left on 174 Ave. To the junction with 7 St. Follow 7 St. to 142 Ave.**
(2) Milton Godard House, 2 1/2 story with gable roof. Gothic arched windows (one is in the north facing gable end.) This house is cross-gabled. NRHP c.1860-65

❖**Stay on 142 Ave., and proceed north to Highway 64. Turn right and head back east to Maquoketa.**
(3) Shadrack Burleson home. 2 story gable roof house with brick addition. 1860

❖**Take Highway 61 north to Hurstville, and the right-hand turn-off to the Hurstville Road,** stopping to visit the four lime kilns.
(4) Hurstville Lime Kilns are significant not only because of the building material used, but also because they represent a major industry in Jackson County in the 19th Century. Completely restored and in some cases rebuilt in the 1980s by local volunteer labor. NRHP 1882

❖**Continue on Hurstville Road. Turn to the left onto Rockdale Road and cross the bridge.** This is the North Fork of the Maquoketa River, which joins the South Fork downstream about a quarter of a mile to become the Maquoketa River. Rockdale Road becomes gravel and to the right you will see a large quarry operation. The quarry was once the site of an Indian village, and later the little town of Rockville prospered here at the time of the mill. On the south rim of the quarry pit is the mill, which once had a large slough and millrace between it and the river.
(5) Tubbs Mill, now roofless and inaccessible. More easily seen in the winter when the trees are bare. 1865

❖**Come back to Maquoketa on the Hurstville Road driving south, cross the bridge over the South Fork and into Maquoketa.**

Note: There are many more limestone buildings in Jackson County not included in these drives. For further information about their whereabouts read the *Survey of Limestone Architecture* available at the town libraries and at the Jackson County Historical Society Museum and Geneology Library at the Fairgrounds in Maquoketa.

South Fork Township Loop

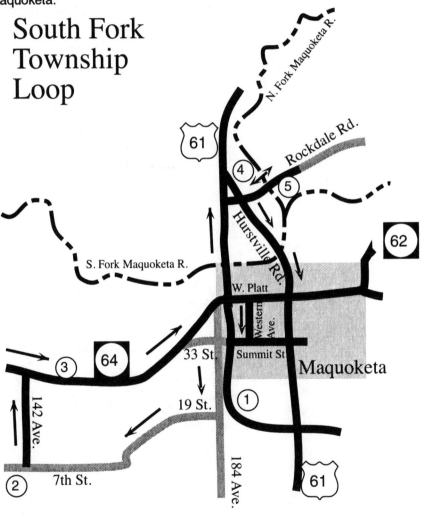

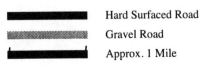

Hard Surfaced Road

Gravel Road

Approx. 1 Mile

Chapter 3

Great Roads of Jackson County

> *"Always beautiful and interesting, in these long days of*
> *mid-July the old road is at its best."*
>
> Some Summer Days in Iowa
> Frederick Lazell, 1909

We continue our exploration of Jackson County by driving on a few of its special roads. I call them "great roads", but I am aware that in comparison to Wolf Creek Pass, Colorado, or the Coastal Highway along the Pacific Ocean in California, these roads are not great in the sense of stupendous scenery. These roads in eastern Iowa, along the bluffs of the Mississippi, in the valleys, and on the ridges, are great in their completeness, their unexpectedness, and their charm.

The roads will take you on several different levels of journeying. They will show you the countryside and its life, but also they may carry you back to the time when settlers first saw the county. Whether you are seeing a stand of oaks or a soaring eagle over the Mississippi, or whether you are seeing with your mind's eye the scenes from our past, is all up to you and your interests.

Secluded and seldom traveled, these great little roads are quiet and offer the opportunity to look beyond our busy lives into another time and into the realm of nature.

What makes a "great road"? To answer that question involves the laying down of a foundation of criteria as a definition of great roads.

❖*Seclusion* is essential, but it is also relative. The distance from noise and busy highways is what I mean by seclusion. Although some of the roads are remote enough to be termed secluded in any part of the midwest, these are not far from civilization, but are less-traveled so that one can stop the car and roll down the window, listen to the birds, smell the woods, and not worry about impeding much traffic.

❖*Trees* are an important ingredient in the recipe for great roads, They supply dappled shade along the way and a nesting place for birds; grapevines twine up into their branches and the wind makes its music in their crowns.

❖*Wildflowers* and plants which draw the eye down to the roadside and away from the rushing, forward progress of our busy world are to be found along all of the roads. Get a guidebook for help in identification and begin the adventure of learning the plants' names. Find out which are indigenous and which are travelers who are happy to make a home here.

❖*Waterways* such as trout streams, brooks and dry gullies, filled only after heavy rains, add to the sense of nature's life. We may alter the course of a stream, but water will always find a way to move, and in its movement it gurgles and splashes and tells its story.

❖*Views and vistas* which open up, ahead, through the trees, or over the high banks of green verges, or between the shoulders of bluffs, are like the pages of a book which promise a wonderful story. If I lived on the top of a ridge in Jackson County I would have a hard time getting my work done, for I would sit at the window and watch the play of sunlight on pasture grass, or the winds dancing through the knee-high corn. The clouds building in the west would have to tell me to run out and get the clothes off the line because a storm might be brewing. A sunset streaming out from behind the billows of pink, piled cumulus clouds would tell me something about the day to come. There is a lifetime of interests in watching the world around us. Driving along with vistas opening ahead is the next best thing to living up on that high ridge.

❖*"Sense of place"* might mean history to some, or anthropology to some, or an inexpressible quality of sunlight to others. Buildings and stories and past lives give us that feeling of sense of place. Farms left abandoned, stone houses, little towns, a sixty year old Chevy sitting out behind the orchard, all these help us to define a place and catalog it in our memories. Calling to mind Jackson County long after a visit here will involve that "sense of place."

❖*Wildlife* is unpredictable, but if you are on a secluded road near sunset, you may very well see a small herd of deer grazing up a little valley where the sun still shines and lights up their bodies with red and golden embossing. A warm day in February will lure the eagles away from the open water below the dam at Bellevue and you may see them soaring along the waterways all throughout the county. The songbirds which migrate along the Mississippi flyway are often seen in the woods along these roads.

❖*Freshness* refers to sights you don't see often, but it also means the unity of topography and the feeling of rightness that accompanies little clusters of things: buildings or plants or rocks. The appeal will be stronger if it is a road that you do not travel everyday.

These words and concepts make up aspects of the charm of the road. When you travel them it will be up to you to really see the beauty and the history. The lives of green things and flying beings and four-footed creatures are going on all around us and to become involved in the land's life is a privilege offered by the secluded roads. If you can capture a "sense of place" you will find the charm of the road. Good luck, and enjoy the wealth of possibilities here in Jackson County.

Old World Charm

239th Avenue, SW of St. Donatus, off Highway 52 and 389th Street

This is a road of impressions, ephemeral and subtle. Along the road, there was a feeling of Old World charm and a sense that time was moving slowly along this stretch of road; colors seemed more captivating and there was an overall sweetness in the air; it felt good to be alive. These are all elusive images to convey to another person, but if you approach this road with a sense of discovery and "romance", [Webster: "picturesque characteristic or nature"] perhaps you will have your own special impressions.

We discovered the road at dusk on an August evening. A clear, pink sky backlit the dark green shoulders of wooded, low bluffs to the west. The road, which hugs the eastern side of the valley, is near the Tete Des Morts stream which flows briskly through the valley, occasionally meandering from side to side.

Up the bluff, and through the trees, are vast pastures, "lawns" where the cows have kept the grass mowed, but not over-grazed. Rock outcroppings, with rugged ledges, contrast with the smooth, green hillsides. A doe and her fawn moved in little hops away from the sound of the car's wheels slowly crunching on the gravel. They stayed close to the understory growth along the fenceline, their colors blending with the limestone and the few leaves that had turned to fall shades of bronze and brown.

Looking to the stream-side meadow in the valley we saw placid cattle standing knee-deep in the lush, emerald grasses. They also watched us, but seemed undisturbed by our presence.

The evening mists swathed the rounded bluffs and flowed up the smaller, lifting valleys. They looked iridescent, pink and blue; like gauzy scarves. The color was also picked out in the dusk by the blossoms of lobelia and the fading beebalm.

A venerable and abandoned limestone house stands near the road. It has no roof, and there is a wall upstairs painted a deep blue, the color often used for the Virgin Mary's robe by medieval Italian painters. That wall seemed like a testament to the immigrant families. It stands as a symbol of the hopes—of prosperity and freedom, the dreams of sturdy homes, clean water and the freshness of a green valley—that drew families to America and on to Iowa.

> "The rock houses were cool in the summer and
> warm in the winter, a cool breeze always caressed
> the hollow in the hot summer evenings."
>   An old-timer's account

I wonder if the people who built that house were content? Had their dreams been realized? Did the generations who lived there feel fulfillment from the valley and their house beside the road?

> *"There are pioneer souls that blaze their paths*
> *Where highways never ran—*
> *But let me live by the side of the road*
> *And be a friend to man."*
> The House By the Side of the Road
> Sam Walter Foss

Gladys Taber, a longtime favorite author, often wrote of her Connecticut home, Stillmeadow. She says this about a house near a road: "In 1690 men built their houses right by the road." She goes on to say that it was practical to be near the stretch of public road one was responsible to maintain, as well as very handy to drive the huge wagonloads of cordwood right up near the house where fuel was needed. Stillmeadow has six "huge" fireplaces. In recent times, however, these houses seem too close to the road. "Occasionally, in our valley, folk have moved the ancient house and set it way back in the woods or on a hill, but I know those houses are not comfortable, since they were not built to be anywhere but right by the road."

There are springs in the eastern bluffs.

> "The wagon trail down into the 'hollow' was sand-
> wiched between the same rolling bluffs and dense
> timber. The creek bubbled along the roadway and
> a stop at the spring for a clear drink of ice water
> refreshed the driver and his passengers."
> An old-timer's account

One small spring by this road courses down and seeps across the road on its way to the stream. It was in just such a spot, on a bright noonday, that John Greenleaf Whittier envisioned his poem, *"Maud Muller"*. His verses seem to capture this valley.

MAUD MULLER
John Greenleaf Whittier

Maud Muller, on a summer's day
Raked the meadow sweet with hay.
Beneath her torn hat glowed the wealth
Of simple beauty and rustic health.
Singing, she wrought, and her merry glee
The mock-bird echoed from his tree.

The Judge rode slowly down the lane,
Smoothing his horse's chestnut mane:
He drew his bridle in the shade
Of the apple-trees, to greet the maid,
And asked a draught from the spring that flowed
Through the meadow across the road.

She stooped where the cool spring bubbled up,
And filled for him her small tin cup,
And blushed as she gave it, looking down
On her feet so bare, and her tattered gown.
"Thanks!" said the Judge, "a sweeter draught
From a fairer hand was never quaffed."

He spoke of the grass, and flowers, and trees,
Of the singing birds and the humming bees;
Then talked of the haying, and wondered whether
The cloud in the west would bring foul weather.

And Maud forgot her brier-torn gown.
And her graceful ankles bare and brown,
And listened, while a pleased surprise
Looked from her long-lashed hazel eyes.

At last, like one who for delay
Seeks a vain excuse, he rode away.
Maud Muller looked and sighed: "Ah, me!"
That I the Judge's bride might be!
He would dress me up in silks so fine,
And praise and toast me at his wine."

The Judge looked back as he climbed the hill,
And saw Maud Muller standing still.
A form more fair, a face more sweet,
Ne'er has it been my lot to meet;
And her modest answer and graceful air
Show her wise and good as she is fair."

"Would she were mine, and I to-day
Like her, a harvester of hay;
No doubtful balance of rights and wrongs,
Nor weary lawyers with endless tongues;
But low of cattle and song of birds,
Health, and quiet, and loving words."

But he thought of his sisters, proud and cold,
And his mother, vain of her rank and gold;
So, closing his heart, the Judge rode on,
And Maud was left in the field alone.
But the lawyers smiled that afternoon,
When he hummed in court an old love-tune;
And the young girl mused beside the well,
Till the rain on the unraked clover fell.

He wedded a wife of richest dower,
Who lived for fashion, as he for power;
Yet oft, in his marble hearth's bright glow,
He watched a picture come and go;
And sweet Maud Muller's hazel eyes
Looked out in their innocent surprise.

Oft when the wine in his glass was red,
He longed for the wayside well instead;
And closed his eyes on his garnished rooms,
To dream of meadows and clover-blooms.
And the proud man sighed, with a secret pain,
"Ah, that I were free again!"
Free as when I rode that day,
Where the barefoot maiden raked her hay."

She wedded a man unlearned and poor,
And many children played round her door;
But care and sorrow and wasting pain
Left their traces on heart and brain.

And oft when the summer sun shone hot
On the new-mown hay in the meadow lot,
And she heard the little spring brook fall
Over the roadside, through the wall,
In the shade of the apple-tree again
She saw a rider draw his rein,
And, gazing down with timid grace,
She felt his pleased eyes read her face.

Alas for maiden, alas for Judge,
For rich repiner and household drudge!
God pity them both! and pity us all,
Who vainly the dreams of youth recall;
For of all sad words of tongue or pen
The saddest are these: "It might have been!"

(Excerpts from the poem)

The soul is fueled with the connections made between literature and nature; between personal experience and imagination. The essence of this road will live with me because I stumbled upon this poem, *"Maud Muller"*; the poetry resonates with truth and clarity because I stumbled upon this road, and had the time to see it.

Goat Prairie

109th Street from Z20 to 100th Street, south of Springbrook

This road is very quiet, with several farms, and a deep ravine—dry on the early evening in September when we first drove past. The west side of the road is forested most of the way, with tangles of understory trees and shrubs. The timber is primarily second-growth, that is, the older and original trees were logged out some years ago and these have grown back too close together. Bigger oaks are crowded in among the younger trees, leading us to think it might have once been prairie and oak savanna. The lack of prairie fire since settlement has allowed the trees to come in where the soil is deep and moist to crowd the original oaks which once stood alone, each in its plot of prairie grass.

> "God's invisible attributes, that is to say, God's ev-
> erlasting power and deity, have been visible, ever
> since the world began, to the eye of reason, in the
> things God has made."
>
> Romans 1:20, *The Bible*

There are rank weeds and scrub growth here and there, but this drive affords an excellent opportunity to see a real prairie remnant from the car. Remember this is private property and should not be trespassed upon. The eastern slope discloses the gravelly soil, rock outcroppings and plants to be found on the dry upland prairie. We identified the short, curled-over goldenrod and prairie dropseed, a bluish-colored clump of short, fountaining grass. We also saw little bluestem with its fuzzy, white seed heads, and the six-foot tall big bluestem that was waving its turkey-foot seed spikes.

It was impossible to tell how far the prairie extended into the upper fields because of a tall bluff leaning over the road in places.

Most available public prairie sites in the county are tallgrass and are not original, but planted and cultivated. But here is a true little remnant, and a tiny representative of the vast prairie that once covered portions of Jackson County.

> *"The prairie grass dividing, its special odor breathing,*
> *I demand of its spiritual corresponding*
> *Those of the open atmosphere,*
> *coarse, sunlit, fresh, nutritious,*
> *Those of earth-born passion,*
> *simple, never constrained, never obediant,*
> *Those of inland America."*
>
> *The Prairie Grass Dividing*
> Walt Whitman

40

Little information is available about these rocky hill prairies sometimes called goat prairies. Let me tell you a little of what I've learned from experiences on them and from visiting with "prairie-folk" like Dr. Ray Hamilton, of Maquoketa.

The prairie biome which covered all of Iowa and portions of the surrounding states came into existence after the last glaciation, or about 8,000 to 12,000 years ago.

Earlier in time, a vast inland sea covered this area and laid down the trillions of sea creatures' shells which became dolomite limestone. In places the soil grew to a depth of many feet, with deep and rich topsoil created by the thick tangle of roots and decaying grasses and plants.

The dry, upland prairie, on the other hand, was covered with glacial gravel, some of it called Windemeer gravel, and thin soil over and around the often visible limestone outcroppings. On this habitat, unique plants developed in a time 3000 to 8000 years ago. And for thousands of years it existed with, and because, of vast herds of roving, grazing animals like the elk and bison, and because of the yearly cleansing prairie fire. Only in the last 150 years of its life has the prairie been threatened, and in the case of the tallgrass prairie, almost destroyed by the settlers' farming techniques. The hill prairies offered little farming use except for light grazing and, therefore, a few survived because of their unattractiveness as cropland. Its main enemies are overgrazing or scraping for gravel, gravel pit operations and encroachment by invasive vegetation like cedar trees, sumac and plum. These trees crowd out the prairie plants which have developed a harmonious relationship on the dry bluffs.

Stand on a dry upland prairie and look down at your feet—about a square foot around them—and you will see plants which you have never seen before, or anywhere else. They are to be found only in this prairie environment. Like the rare alpine plants of the European mountains that are so highly prized for rock gardens, these plants are especially adapted to their unique home, and just as rare.

There are many kinds of sedges, a type of grass-like plant that is low to the ground with sawtooth blade edges. ("Sedges have edges.") Sedges also have interestingly shaped blossoms. The rock sandwort that look like a brownish moss with tiny white blossoms waving above the pad of foliage, are so small they are easily overlooked, but exquisite in form. Black lichen covers the gravel and tiny bones of animals litter the powdery dry soil between the rocks. Petite orchids reward some prairies with their presence.

Blooming plants live on the prairie in successions of neighborhoods. There are birdsfoot violets which appear in early May, their low blossoms covering the prairie bluffs with a blue haze.

The downy painted cup and yellow hoary puccoon usher in the summer heat, and the pale purple coneflowers, a species of echinacea, and spiked lobelia of early July are visited by what seem to be hundreds of fritillaries. These butterflies can

41

fly from one plant to another because the flowers grow on a single spike, but in vast drifts of the same variety of plant.

August brings the most intense color with the rough blazing star, its blooms are hot pink. This variety of the liatris is not usually found in the plant guides, but it is identified by its burst of bloom at the end of a two-foot stalk. The many asters begin to make a show in August.

As the summer days pass, so do these bright spots of color, to be replaced with the low goldenrod and the white ladies' tresses orchid.

Unless you are a student of prairie flora, most of these varieties are new to you. They do, however, exist—even without our awareness. There they are, perhaps near a gravel pit or an old railroad right-of-way, or in a neglected cemetery. But you need to know what you are seeing, or they might appear to be just a patch of rough and neglected ground. Not wasteland; prairie!

> *"Study nature as the countenance of God"*
>
> Kingsley

Always, on the prairie, are the grasses. Last year's dead grasses form a clump or mat from which the new grasses spring. In June they are greening up and by September they are seeding out. Around each clump of grass and each plant is a space of bare ground. Although the dry upland prairie plants live in community and depend on the soil chemistry created by their neighbors, they don't live in each other's pockets. No crowding here. Careful walkers can pick their way through the grasses on the gravel and the dry soil in most places.

On a warm June day the temperature in your backyard may be around 85 degrees, while on the prairie, even with a good breeze, it feels like 95 degrees. Prairies are hot during midday. The heat, radiated back from all the rock just below the surface, and all the gravel and outcroppings, suits the grasses and plants just fine, and they seem to thrive on these extreme conditions.

The prairie has a special smell unlike any other place I have ever known. It is a clean and astringent scent. The dead grasses produce a sweet smell even in November. The scent of the pesky cedar trees, which love the dry uplands, reminds one just a little of the West. The subtle perfumes of flowers such as the state flower, the wild rose, or the pungent yellow prairie coneflower are uniquely blended.

The air feels drier on a prairie. Even after a rain, the water drains away quickly. This biome relies on good and speedy drainage. The plants don't transplant well, but sometimes seed themselves along the sides of gravel roads. You may see puccoon, yellow coneflower and big bluestem far away from a prairie site.

The color of the prairie in the winter, when everything is dormant, is cinnamon. If a reddish mist appears over an old pasture, you know there are some prairie grasses in it, especially the blades of little bluestem. In its growing season it has streaks of red along each grass blade, and in the dormant stage remains slightly rufous.

Dean Roosa and the late Sylvan Runkel, both Iowa plant authorities, wrote several guidebooks to Iowa wildflowers. In their collaboration called *Wildflowers of the Tallgrass Prairie*, they admonish us as follows: "Please remember that prairies can be miserably hot places with no shade for an escape. But they can also be among the most peaceful places on earth if visited early, before the sun becomes punishing, or late, when the wind has died with the setting sun."

There are not many dry hill prairies left and if you know of one, protect it. Don't overgraze it and don't scrape it for the gravel; it is really too precious. It is a survivor, carrying on its well-regulated existence even in the midst of invasive modern life. To me it is like a garden planted by an old god or goddess; it remains, and it can tell us of a time before our kind walked this land.

Mississippi Bottoms and Bluffs
500 Avenue from Highway 52 to Green Island

This road begins at the intersection of the highway and the gravel road leading past Reeseville Cemetery. The graveyard with its cedar trees has some very old headstones and some interesting newer ones also. To the north of the mown lawns of the cemetery, along the ditches, are ferns still glowing green on September 15th and bright blue lobelia blooming among the pale lavender, white, and vibrantly purple, asters. Clumps of the prairie grass big bluestem flourish near the graveled edges of the road, part soil and part gravel. We wonder where the seeds have blown in from as there seem to be no prairie remnants nearby.

About a quarter of a mile into the road you should begin to watch to the east, on your right, for glimpses of the spectacular view of the Mississippi River plain known as the Green Island Bottoms. There are several spots that cry out for a bench! To sit and look out over the shallow waters, channels and aquatic plants which create a tapestry of many shades of color would be so very good.

Eventually you will come to a fork in the road. The left is a lane to a farmstead, the right is a 'B' level or low maintenance road. Don't attempt this 'B' level if it's raining or snowing; it is very steep and mostly dirt with some protruding ledges of limestone.

There is a feeling of isolation here that inspires images of weathered faces and buckskin shirts and breeches.

> "Let us picture in imagination the history of the Great Valley of the Mississippi a splendid drama enacted upon a giant stage which reaches from the Alleghenies to the Rockies and from the Great Lakes to the Gulf of Mexico and through which the Father of Waters sweeps majestically. Let us people this stage with real men and women - picturesque red men and no less interesting white men, Indians, Spaniards, Frenchmen, Englishmen, explorers, warriors, priests, voyageurs, coureurs du bois, fur traders, and settlers. Let the scenes be set about the lakes, along the rivers, among the hills, on the plains, and in the forests. Then, viewing this pageant of the past, let us write the true tales of the Great Valley as we write romance— with life, action, and color - that the history of our Great Valley may live."
>
> *The Man with the Iron Hand*
> John Carl Parish, 1913

44

If one dared, and the emergency brake was good, this would be a place to stop the car and get out and listen to the forest, smell it, and feel the moisture of its greenness upon one's face. This would be a place to let imagination conjure up the past peoples just mentioned. Be sure, however, to pull on the brake—this road is steep!

Traveling on, the road passes ledges and loose limestone rubble, all shaded with a dense and quite high tree canopy; it is nearly dark under its many leaves.

Then, suddenly, the road becomes a street in Green Island, emerging from the trees between two houses! To come from the isolation of the dark forest immediately into the bright sunshine of mowed lawns and asphalt driveways is quite a jolt!

Have you ever wondered what a road up through the forested bluffs along the Mississippi would be like? Here is a chance to visit one.

Bluff and Riverine World

123rd Avenue off Highway 64; a dead end.

This little country road, with a few houses along it, branches off from the intersection known as Buckhorn. A few hundred yards west of the gravel road is the original Buckhorn Tavern operated by Shadrack Burleson back in the 1850s when immigrants by the thousands passed this way.

The scenery along the southern stretch of this road reminds one of the mid-19th century, with the rough pastures, the meandering stream and the gently curving road. Behind the quarry is an interesting old saltbox house, part of a village called Joinerville, and farther along, a steep bank of limestone once afforded a sloping, little farmyard for hogs. A farmstead is tucked into the ledges there even now. Newer homes on the west side of the road blend in well with their rustic setting.

The road lifts here briefly and around a curve is more pasture and thin woodlands. Along the fence grow wild grape and bittersweet vines. There are bluebird houses on the fenceposts.

The way of the road slips downhill and we enter the shadow of tall bluffs to the west, covered with mature trees. In the spring, often before any other place, there are wildflowers to be seen here.

These bluffs are off-limits for walkers, they are too sheer and the soil is only a fragile frosting over the bedrock. But farther along, after the bridge crossing Pumpkin Run Creek, is a small conservation park called Joinerville. Here beside the broad and serene Maquoketa River the bluffs are more easily accessible. There are log steps leading up to a picnic meadow, with water pump, overlooking the river through the trees, and on these lower bluffs are wildflowers to walk among.

In the boat ramp area you can spy the wood duck houses placed high up on the tree trunks, and sometimes there are yellow buttercups blooming in the grass and even in the tire tracks.

Now, in September, the river is low and placid. The trees on the opposite bank are reflected in the limpid water, and look like an imagined canvas entitled, "Trees and Water Trees", by some Impressionistic painter. It is so still today that at times the reflection is as clear as the actual trees, a perfect mirror image. The banks of the river are low and level and one feels a part of the riverine world. A distant splash, followed by the receding 'V' in the water, is probably a muskrat returning to its bank nest upstream. Overhead the soft blue sky is a backdrop for the slow circling of five turkey vultures cruising on the updrafts off the bluffs behind us.

46

This is a dead-end road, so we turn around and retrace our route. Along the road, in ditches and on the bluffs are the bright and deep purple asters known as New England asters. If the plants stand in the bright autumn sunshine they are hung with Monarch butterflies looking like an altogether odd, purple Christmas tree decorated with orange angels. The cabbage and sulphur butterflies, with fluttering wings of white or yellow, twinkle and shimmer when seen from a distance.

The tall bushy asters could be the equivalent of an autumn Christmas tree, just bring them into your living room and decorate them with artificial Monarchs and yellow and white fairy lights. Quite lovely, but the real thing is bound to be better. Get out and see it.

A red-tailed hawk lifts off a branch just as the car passes, and for a few seconds we see it level with our car window. It pumps free of Earth's gravity and after a half-dozen muscular downstrokes of its broad wings it glides effortlessly over the pasture, its shadow waltzing among the yellow goldenrod and lavender shaving-brush bristles of the Canadian thistle.

Fall is so near. Here and there an intensely colored tree draws us on, tantalizing us with images of the weeks to come. Although it is not quite ready to burst upon us here in the country, every street in town has a maple with a huge branch of buttery yellow leaves and the Marshall ash have gone eggplant in their crowns. The flower beds glow with mums of every shade. The dahlias and marigolds seem oblivious to the nighttime chill. The morning glories are just getting up a full head of steam to really bloom— big, blue trumpets of flowers.

The grass of lawn and meadow seems lusher than ever, so green, and with an intensity heightened by the rays of a lower sun.

We've passed the full moon without a frost, so who knows how long the nicotiana and pansies will bloom on—perhaps until Thanksgiving. Imagine the Thanksgiving feast set out on the diningroom table—the bowls and platters of fine food, the plates and glasses gleaming—all on a snowy white, linen tablecloth. Autumn's colors are displayed here: the platter with its crispy, brown roasted turkey, bowls of orange, whipped squash, yellow scalloped corn, ruby red cranberry sauce, and the faithful, purple pansies in an old, green glass vase. What an array of harvest bounty.

The pansies are such hardy little souls, that I've picked them on Christmas Day from under an insulating snow.

A great road and a mind's journey can lead from the springtime of pristinely white Dutchmen's breeches, through a bright summer of black-eyed Susans, to Autumn's purple pansies, and circle back to end with a vision of the white stillness of snow on a Christmas Day.

Ferns

182nd Avenue off E17

A half a mile off busy Highway 61 is this quiet little road. Along its edges are some of my favorite green and growing things— ferns. There are ferns growing on many roads in Jackson County, but I have never seen so many different kinds in such a short distance. There are maidenhair and large cinnamon fern, perhaps lady fern or silvery spleenwort.

Ferns, which are a non-flowering plant, are identified by their spore patterns. Fern leaves or fronds unroll from curled fiddleheads and the spores are produced on the underside of the frond. It is so difficult to identify them, especially from the car! I just enjoy the diversity and imagine the many names fitting with the many ferns.

It has been a cool summer, and one must wonder if such a bounty of ferns in September is a phenomenon of the coolness. The years of excess rainfall since the Great Flood Year in Iowa of 1993 may have also been a contributing factor.

The ferns feather the slope on the south side of the road. Perhaps this is an algific slope, always cooler than the surroundings. Dr. Ray Hamilton has this to say about algific slopes in *History of Jackson County, Iowa,* 1989:

> "The oldest living descendants in the county inhabit some areas called cold air (algific) slopes, adjacent to streams in several locations. These unique plant and animal communities receive cool air throughout the summer, transmitted from underlying bedrock, through crevices and sinkholes. Several plant and animal species once thought to be extinct have survived in these locations since glacial times. These communities, discovered within the last decade, are among the rarest and most unique in the midwest."

I doubt that this road's biosystem meets the criteria for an algific slope, but the diversity of ferns is in itself very unique.

On both sides of the road are bluffs and tall trees. In places the road is being eroded and there are steep ravines at its edge. A tall maple leaning over the road should be spectacular in October.

We identified thimbleweed, evening primrose, white snakeroot, and an unusual grass, possibly porcupine grass. Even though this is not typical prairie, some of the native plants have found a stable home here. One of the difficult aspects of identifying the prairie plants of the region is that few guidebooks address themselves to the short grass prairie. The diversity of prairie plants is sometimes daunting when it comes to pasting a label on a plant blooming right there at your feet, but not to be found in the photographs or illustrations in the guides. And some are just recently "discovered" and too "new" to be in the books. Of course, they are not new, but are only the current generation of species which may have flourished near that spot for thousands of years, just undiscovered by us Euro-Americans. Euro-Americans, that's how my daughters, the anthropologists, refer to those of us whose great-grandparents came from Europe.

This road is quiet and reminiscent of roads they might have traveled, those great-grandparents of ours. Did they appreciate the freshness, the new plants which they had never seen before? Do we?

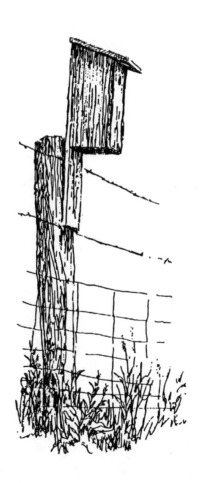

Chapter **4**

"I Just Washed The Car"

GREAT EXCUSE. . .

It goes something like this. . .

"Honey, let's go for a ride. Let's take a lunch and find one of these *Great Roads* I've been reading about in this book. What do you think?"

"Sounds super, dear, but I just washed the car, and you know those roads are all gravel and dusty. Sorry."

"But, sweetie, here on page 58 it says there are some really nifty sights to see from hard-surfaced roads, too."

"Oh, really! Well, in that case, sugar, let's get that lunch packed, put in some Willie Nelson tapes, or if Iowa's playing today we can listen on the radio, and hit the road!"

You see how it goes? In any case, don't let a clean car stop you from seeing the sights of Jackson County.

"I Just Washed The Car Drive" #1
Mid-central and southeast county

This drive is on hard-surfaced roads which take in outstanding vistas, rock outcroppings, oak savannas and some of the prettiest farm land in the world.

❖**From Maquoketa head north on Highway 61**, crossing the South Fork of the Maquoketa just outside town, and the North Fork south of Fulton. The rocky gorge here is always a good indication of the river's level; when it is low the limestone streambed is visible, but when the water level is high, the river really rolls and tumbles through the gorge.

❖**Turn east on E17 towards Andrew**. If you've been camping at the Caves, you could take the Caves Road, 428, north out of the park to where it meets E17, you will cross Highway 61 heading east to Andrew. Both 428 and E17 have been designated as *Iowa Scenic Byways*.

❖**At Andrew find E17 at the south edge of town and proceed to Springbrook**. This section of the drive has a spectacular hill which really "impressed" the bikers on "RAGBRAI" several years ago. It is a curving, long haul. Springbrook will treat you to the small-town neatness of its buildings and yards. Gawk at the stone Gonner General Store, which is empty right now, but a great building, nonetheless.

❖**Continue on through Springbrook on E17 until the junction with Z34, turn south and head to Preston.** Preston is one of the newest towns in Jackson County, being platted in the 1870s. It has an interesting business district with some shops worth checking out.

❖**Now proceed east on Highway 64, past Miles, to Sabula.** Be sure to stop at the Jackson County Welcome Center and step into the "old" one-room replica schoolhouse, which has a modern conference room upstairs, clean and modern indoor rest rooms and a gift shop of local crafts and art in the basement. Tourist information is available on the first floor, as well as old school desks and blackboard. And don't miss ringing the old bell—pull the rope and hear the pealing of the bell from the cupola.

Here, at Sabula, are some great spots for shoreline fishing: Driscoll Island, right by the Highway going into this Island City; and the backwater lakes that surround the town. If you are planning to continue east, exit the state by way of the causeway north out of town, and onto the bridge across the Mississippi. The causeway is special because it is right over the shallow backwaters, with egrets perched in the treetops, waterlilies blooming in still waters fished by Great blue herons, and fallen trees perfect for whole families of sunning turtles.

In April, the trees along the causeway near the bridge approach are dotted with the nests of the Great Blue Heron. The nests are near the tops of the trees, sometimes 20 in one tree. We counted as many as 200 twig nests, each with its sentinel heron guarding the eggs. This rookery is a crowded, but tranquil community. On the same day we saw about 20 pelicans in the waters north of Driscoll Island. A very large and impressive bird.

A car ferry is sometimes running to Savannah, Illinois, just across the Mississippi, during the summer months.

❖**If you are returning to Maquoketa come back by way of Bellevue, and Highway 52**, *The* Great *River Road*, which outlines the eastern boundary of Iowa. At Bellevue take Highway 62, *The Ansel* Briggs *Highway*, back to Andrew and then Maquoketa.

Make a day of it and pack a lunch to eat at Driscoll Island or at Bellevue State Park. Or go spur-of-the-moment and stop to eat in a restaurant along the way.

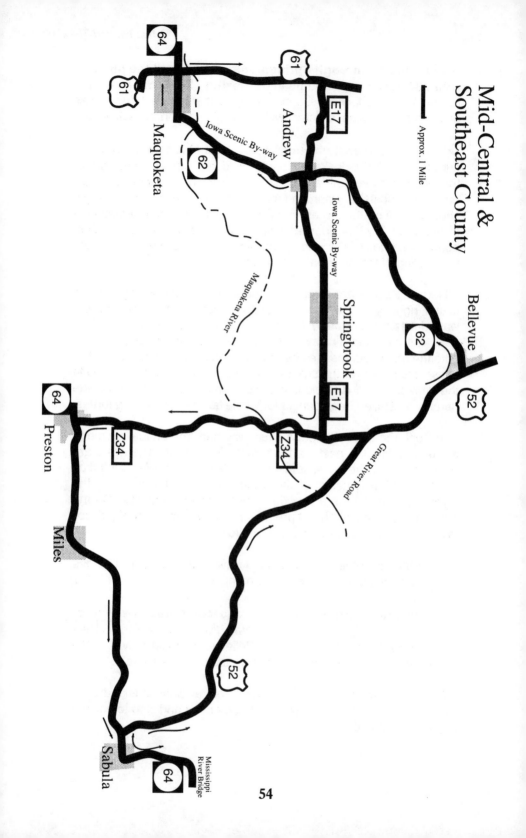

Mid-Central &
Southeast County

— Approx. 1 Mile

64

61

61

Maquoketa

Iowa Scenic By-way

62

Andrew

E17

Iowa Scenic By-way

Springbrook

Maquoketa River

Bellevue

62

52

E17

64

Preston

Z34

Z34

Great River Road

Miles

52

Sabula

64

Mississippi River Bridge

Of Roads...#1
Map Lines

Look at a map of Jackson County. The lines that represent roads on the map are of three distinct types. The rarest is the perfectly straight line, it represents a road laid out on the section lines. Such roads are more common farther west on the flat Iowa farmland. Much more common here, are the gentle curves of the second type of road—the ridge road. Most paved roads in Jackson County are ridge roads. The squiggles of the valley roads, which follow a stream bed, are the third type. One look at the map tells you where valley becomes ridge.

The ridge road offers a spectacular vista of timbered valley after timbered valley receding into the blue haze of the distance, like a porcelain lithophane.

On either side, are the well-cared for farm fields with their contrasting contours of hay and corn. We may be known as a "poor" county on a state level and in comparison with the flat fields of central Iowa, but I'm beginning to think it a well-kept secret that our fields look very prosperous. And the fields are so satisfyingly laid out. For example, those along the road from Andrew to Bellevue, are like a landscaped garden, with contrasts in color, texture and form. How proud their husbandfolk must be of them, for their beauty is accompanied by the knowledge that the contour plowing and terracing and the strip planting is good for yields and the environment. This type of conservation farming stops soil erosion, and it pleases the eye as well— functional art!

The electrical wires along the roads provide perches for swallows at eveningtime. Winter afternoons find sparrowhawks every quarter mile or so and red-tailed hawks every half mile. (They seem to hunt in each other's territory without confrontation.) Soaring overhead, so high that it is hard to identify them, are the turkey vultures and eagles. (Check a bird book for the silhouette of their wing shapes for identification.) As they descend, on a down-draught, watch for the distinctive white head and tailfeathers of the eagle. If three or four big birds are soaring and circling high up over the fields they are most likely turkey vultures.

What a change there is from the open ridge roads to the twisty valley roads, often overshadowed by trees. The shoulders thick with tall wildflowers and shrubs like viburnum, elderberry and honeysuckle. Cardinals swoop ahead of the car, and sometimes a deer may bound out, or a turkey sail across to the woods on the other side of the road.

Up on the ridge road the wind pushes and pulls at the car; down in the valley, all is still. Stop and roll down the window, listen and hear the wind in the tops of the trees. As the afternoon advances, the light is blocked from the valley, while up on the ridge road, the sun is setting unobstructed in a blaze of gold turning to pink, and finally, deep purple clouds. There are days when the sun's rays stream

55

out from behind tall, white thunderheads, so radiantly, that the scene seems to beg for a brass quintet to accompany the glory of its majesty.

After sunset, watch for the full moon rising in a sudden surprise of round, smiling benevolence. It floats so effortlessly over the hills to the east, reminding us of the harvest moon of old and of the peasant farmers working under its light.

Jackson County's map and landscape is filled with curving, squiggly, rounded lines and in the landscape one sees round hills and shallow valleys. The roundness, is to me, a good thing. I very much like the idea that I live surrounded with nature's designs rather than the straight lines of a ruler drawn on a perfectly flat landscape, or the square outline of skyscrapers. Give me "round" any day, even if it means slower driving— round is good for the soul.

"I Just Washed The Car Drive" #2
Northeast county

This drive is highlighted by the little towns you pass through, and along the way is some of the most gorgeous scenery in the Midwest.

❖**From Andrew go north on Highway 62 until the left turn onto Y61.** We are really up on the ridge here, with views to east and west. The road passes the new buildings of the Jackson County Care Facility on the west which replaced the original brick buildings of the old county poor farm. The old Stone Asylum for the Insane is on the right. NRHP

❖**Continue on to LaMotte.** This is a pretty little village. I very much like its square, with the church to the east, a building to the south that may have been a hotel, and the stores to the west. In the center is the picnic shelter, a dry streambed crossed by a footbridge and picnic tables and playground equipment. The railroad depot, restored and well-cared for, sits on a deadend—the most westerly street leading out of the square to the south. It is the only narrow gauge depot in Iowa and on the National Registry of Historic Places. The narrow gauge railroad used this depot from 1879 to the 1930s. A beautiful valley setting.

❖**Leave LaMotte on D55.** The road is another ridge climber and dips and curves gently amid the broad vistas. On old maps, this road was known as the *Cascade to Gordon's Ferry Wagon Road*.
When it joins Highway 52, turn left and go north into St. Donatus. The old world charm of St. Donatus can be felt even before getting

56

into the village; it is here on this highway. The rounded bluffs on either side shelter the road and make it feel like a part of a long valley in Europe.

❖**Backtrack on Highway 52 through Bellevue; take Z15 to Springbrook.** Looking at the same views from the opposite direction affords the opportunity to see the exact sights but with different lighting and perspective. Watch for the birch trees along the Mississippi River bluffs north of Bellevue. They are rarely found in Iowa and then only in the northeast, this is the southern extent of their range. The road to Springbrook is a pleasant drive with lots of scenery and gracious old farmsteads.

❖**At Springbrook take E17 back to Andrew.** This area was known to settlers as "Seldom Seen" because folks who lived in these deep valleys of Brush Creek had no through road to town. They just opened gates and traveled across pastures and fields, up bluffs and down. It was an arduous trip, so they didn't make it often. Thus they were "seldom seen" in town. Isn't it nice to have this lovely road through the heart of it? The bluffs, valleys and the trout stream give it real ambiance.

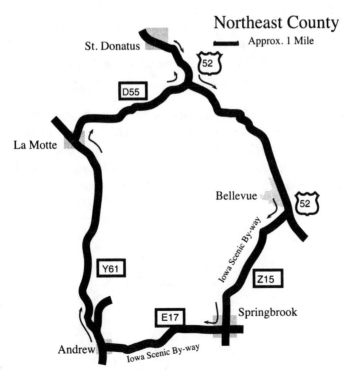

Northeast County

Of Roads...#2

Not Flat!

I have a friend who has a love affair with highways. The strong allure of smooth cement and the potential for speed is captivating. He loves to get in his big car and swoop along, pushing the speed limit. Perhaps the Jurassic-sized earthmovers and the mammoth cement-layers which prepared the roadbed, have left an aura of power, attracting him on some subliminal level. Even my friend, however, admits that along the efficient new four-lane north and south of Maquoketa too much has been cleared away; trees, farms and old schoolhouses that once gave this drive character.

Many people who travel through Iowa on Interstate 80 think the state is "empty", but that's because the Interstate traverses the state on a path-of-least-resistance. An English acquaintance, who flew into Sioux City, Iowa, from Minneapolis, felt that Iowa was nothing but flat farm fields. In explaining that the north central portion of the state had been glaciated, really scoured, in the most recent times geologically speaking, he looked at me with pitying indulgence. To me his look suggested his thoughts—"Poor thing, she thinks the Loess Hills are topographically comparable to the Welsh Mountains."

But, dear John, you need to come drive around Jackson County where the most recent glaciation did not occur. Here the slopes are dotted with limestone outcroppings, and bluffs are head and shoulders above deep valleys, and the ridgelines offer a view that recedes into Delft-blue mists. Roads go up steep hills and down slithery gravel roads. And here are trees—oak savannas and hickory-groves, sugar maple, basswood and black walnut; the fruiting trees, shrubs and vines which make every bit of waste timber a place fit for wildlife kings and queens. Our corn and soybean fields share their abundance with deer, birds and ducks, before being harvested and shared with the world. The ring-necked pheasants live in the lap of the Goddess of bounty, and so do we.

"I Just Washed The Car Drive" # 3
Northwest county

This drive has both the wide open spaces and the limestone ledges that the county showcases. From the shaded valleys of the Maquoketa Caves State Park to the sunny fields of Garryowen is quite a change in scenery.

❖**From Maquoketa go north on Highway 64 to the Caves Road, 428, going past the Caves State Park entrance and on to E17.** This route, a rather twisty ridge road most of the way, has interesting houses and things to do and see. There are several antiquing possibilities and a country cafe. And there will soon be a museum opened at the entrance of the Caves State Park. And, of course, there are the Caves.

❖**Take E17 left to Y31 north, the Bernard Road, to Garryowen.** Garryowen's St. Patrick Catholic Church is a limestone building built in 1853 with a later belltower addition. This is the oldest church building in the Dubuque Archdiocese; the second oldest parish (1840) in the Archdiocese; and the oldest rural Catholic parish in the state of Iowa. NRHP. The cemetery north of the church is filled with the names of the Irish immigrants who settled this area in the late 1840s.

❖**At Garryowen turn back south on Y31 until D61, the Bellevue-Cascade Road, and then east to Otter Creek.** Another limestone church is just west of Otter Creek on this road; St. Lawrence Catholic Church, built in 1883. There is good scenery along the way. A curving Lytles Creek, with its ledges on one side and low, green banks on the other, keeps some areas quite remote.

❖**From Otter Creek proceed east on D61 to Cottonville.** Some interesting farmsteads and oak savannas are to be seen. Cottonville was on the stage road from Davenport to Dubuque, by way of Andrew, in the early 1840s.

❖**From Cottonville turn south on Y61 to E17 just north of Andrew. Proceed to Highway 62 and come south to Maquoketa.** This northwest segment of the county is less populated, and has few towns. The good farm land continues to draw those who live here.

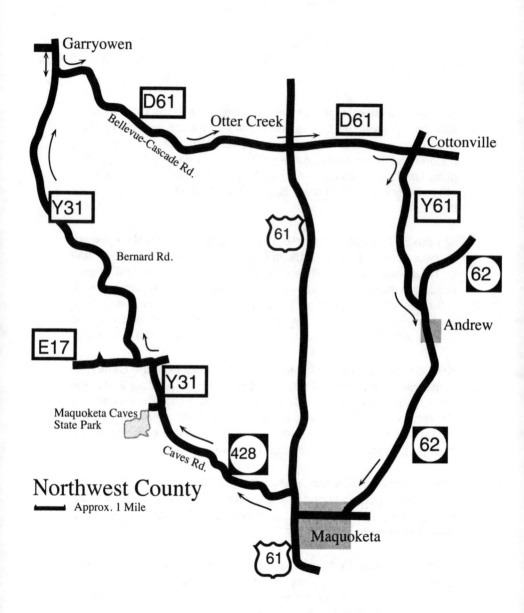

Garryowen

D61

Bellevue-Cascade Rd.

Otter Creek

D61

Cottonville

Y31

61

Y61

Bernard Rd.

62

E17

Andrew

Y31

Maquoketa Caves
State Park

62

Caves Rd.

428

Northwest County
Approx. 1 Mile

Maquoketa

61

Of Roads...# 3

Winter

It was an early winter. Fall was hardly begun before very cold, windy, icy and snowy weather slipped into the Midwest. Thanksgiving Day brought a "warm-up" to 32 degrees. (Nevertheless, we did still have a whole vase of pansies from the flower garden. As I say—they are hardy souls!)

When the snow covers the land a great change is worked, because suddenly, the view is opened up and one's perception is deepened. In the distance what seems like a paper-cutting creation of five black trees on three white hills is back-lit by a pink sky. Mere trees, against a gentle rise, become works of art. The four, poised deer in the harvested field are cunning sculptures until they bound away.

The foundation of a small house huddles, sunken and crumbly, against a rise in a rough valley. Nearby are dark snags of multiflora rose bushes and the tall, dead stalks of goldenrod.

As the sun strikes across the road, the bare trees along a bluff are burnished, copper and bronze, and the layered levels of limestone seem like seats in a Greek amphitheater. Through the misty, sparkling cold air, one can imagine a day in Greece: a goatboy plays his panpipes and calls his flock to make way for the actors in their masks. Comedy or tragedy?—wait and see.

The wind turns the pinwheel of the windmill, but it brings up no water; it has been disconnected for years. The metal shaft, rusty and clanging in the wind, swings free from the pump—no more work to do. It is now a perch for pigeons, and in the summer, daredevil kids, who climb up to the high platform to see "all the way to Davenport".

Now, amid the drifts, can be seen the rare, big boulders left by a retreating lobe of glacier. It dipped an icy toe into our county a million years ago, and left behind its detritus of rocks when it receded. The dried pods of milkweed peak out from the boulders, looking futuristic—like pincers on rods. The cattails are opening to fluff and the stiff winter winds carry away the white down, it settles gently on the snow. Ice crystals form on the fluff, like diamonds on white fur, against white shoulders.

Come out in early winter and see the bare bones of the woods and the soft white shoulders of the hills.

I Just Washed The Car Drive #4

Southwest county

The land on this drive has the feel of history about it. Vanished settlements, Indian sites, the river, and the awesome scenery are the special attractions.

❖**From Maquoketa go west on Highway 64 to Baldwin.** This is part of the Anamosa Wagon Road. When the highway was widened in the early 1980s, it lost a good bit of its character and charm, but it still has interesting scenery and farms along its way. Don't overlook Buckhorn as you whiz by.

❖**At Baldwin turn north on Y34 to Emeline.** This might have been part of Clark Road, an early trail from Buffalo, a settlement south of Davenport, to Dubuque.

❖**From Emeline go east on E17 to Iron Hill, and on to Y53, Esgate Road.** This is a high ridge road with farm ponds, timber and fields on both sides.

❖**Take the Esgate Road to Maquoketa, it will join Highway 61 at Hurstville.** Esgate Road was built in the late 1980s as a farm-to-market road. I think the engineers did a fine job of making a well-designed highway, and still retaining some of the character of the landscape. The curves are gentle and it's an interesting road to drive.

❖**At Hurstville exit Highway 61 onto the Hurstville Road and return to Maquoketa.** The Hurstville Road takes you past the Lime Kilns and through the old company town of Hurstville. The old iron bridge over the South Fork just at the north edge of the Maquoketa city limits will probably be replaced in the very near future. Drive over it while you can, there are fewer and fewer of these structures left.

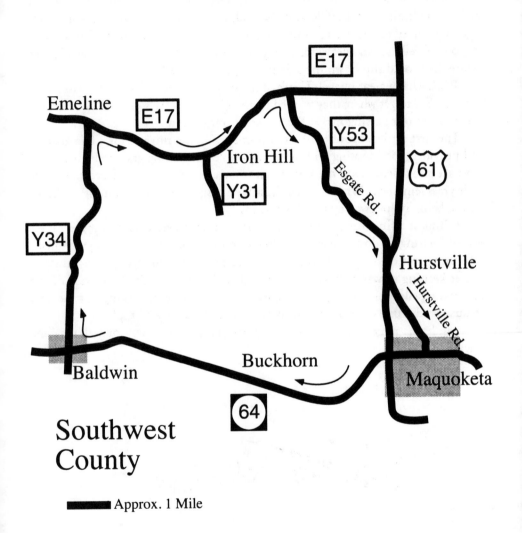

Emeline E17

E17

Iron Hill

Y53

Y31

Esgate Rd.

61

Y34

Hurstville

Hurstville Rd.

Buckhorn

Baldwin

Maquoketa

Southwest
County

64

Approx. 1 Mile

Of Roads...#4

The Track

I have a sense that the ridge roads are very ancient tracks once traveled by prehistoric Indians, by buffalo and elk, and, by the woolly mammoth—the Stone Age elephant of the American continent. It's just logical to assume travelers would stay out of wetlands and heavy forests if possible and walk along the narrow ridgeline where they could slip down the side if danger threatened.

Walk, what a great image! Think of the past time when all footed creatures on earth *walked* to get where they wanted to go. Now we move so fast in our cars, the breeze from our passing makes the grasses shimmer and wave.

The first settlers drove their oxen teams along the ridge roads. The gravelly soil provided good footing and there was ample nourishing grass to be nipped if the pace slackened. Soon the stagecoach came along and the road became dusty; little grass remained. When the stage rumbled past, a cloud of dust hung in the air before being swept away by the ridge winds.

I think it a fine thing to remember those earlier travelers and to respect their way of "getting on down the road." Now we cruise that road; radio playing music, refreshing soft drink in the holder, air conditioner keeping us cool in summer, heater keeping us warm in winter, tinted glass shutting out the harsh rays of the sun and repelling the biting and stinging insects, headlights picking out the deer at dusk, and cruise control regulating the speed at a steady 55 mph.

Yes, let us remember those former travelers, and their way of walking "the track."

A Day on the Prairie
Off Codfish Hollow Road

Spring prairie foliage, not so very tall, we weren't really lookin', for trouble anyhow
    we should have known not, to amble through the prairie,
        guess we thought we knew what we were lookin' for

All fanned out, walkin' through the grasses, saying ahh– to this plant, ahh– to that
    an older woman saw him, she seemed to keep composure,
        but as I said, we really weren't expectin' this at all

Dark brown snake, lying by a boulder, loosely coiled in the sun, quite content
    head puffed like a rattler, vaguely looked familiar,
        all our hearts were poundin', we were quite intent

Nowhere to hide, our beady eyes explored him, human tongues disgusted him, lickin' our lips
    looked a moment at us, rolled his eyelids backwards,
        shut his eyes from the world, took a little nap

Owner of the land, said he had an interest, meeting all the creatures, on his land
    looked, then with a quickness, reached and grabbed his hands on,
        firm behind the head, and one upon the tail

Snake he didn't like it, eager for a struggle, looked to be a really fine wrestlin' match
    hissed all of his breath out, but didn't sound a warnin',
        rattle might have left him, in a previous bout

Quiet knowledge, stated by a neighbor, Eastern Hognose was the name he bore
    but even this honor, didn't quiet the reptile,
        he wanted let go of and wanted it now

Vomit erupted, all over startled owner, caught him broadside, and head to toe
    warm digesting gray vole. the snake had thrown his supper,
        he got his wish, and was let down, to slide away

Spring prairie foliage, not so very tall, we weren't really lookin', for trouble anyhow
    we should have known not, to amble through the prairie,
        guess we thought we knew what we were lookin' for

Charles Jorgensen

Chapter 5

Of Barns, Windmills, Schools and More

Through the ample open door
of the peaceful country barn,
A sunlit pasture field with cattle and horses feeding,
And haze and vista, and the far horizon falling away.
                                                      A Farm Picture
                                              Walt Whitman, 1865

THINGS TO WATCH FOR ON A DRIVE

There are so many things to see on a drive, and each person has particular favorites. Even a routine drive—one that is made daily, can become fasci nating if categories of things are sought out. For example: count windmills; search out the name of a little stream; find farmhouses from the 1870s. One day may be perfect for counting jet contrails and another perfect for viewing massive "windjammer" clouds sailing ahead of the wind.

See the ordinary, the everyday, with a connoisseur's eye. [Webster's dictionary defines a connoisseur as "one who enjoys with discrimination and appreciation."] Instead of fine wine or rare artworks, become an expert on the unappreciated beauty of the common.

BARNS

Americans are enchanted by barns. A barn draws the eye because of its sheer size; it seems to loom on the horizon. And a barn is a richly sensuous place. All the five senses are used when around a barn: the red of its boards pleases the eye; the sound of the milk pinging into the pail charms the ear; the smell of the blend of ripe hay, warm milk, and sweet manure fills the nose; the feel of the smooth post, rubbed to a shiny patina by many large, four-legged animals, lies polished under the hand; the taste of milk, squirted from the cow's teat into a little visitor's wide-opened mouth, is bursting with flavor. To sit on a three-legged milking stool with head resting on a cow's warm and rough flank, being swished with a tail occasionally, hearing the milk ping and then swoosh as the pail fills, the radio playing cowboy songs and polkas from the dusty window ledge— is to have a rich sensory experience. Do these experiences still exist? I hope so.

There are so many barns in the nation's midsection because they were built as working buildings, needed where the temperatures are cold. They provide shelter for crop storage, cattle and horses, and for processing food. The barn's existence relies on serving these needs. It was said in the television program, "Iowa: An American Portrait," that when the work horse "went", the barns were never the same.

68

Iowa may, in fact, have fewer than her share of barns; many have been pulled down to clear more land for crops. She is so productive that little soil can be wasted on superfluous buildings. Nevertheless, as you drive around this part of Iowa, Jackson County, you will see many barns. You will see some very old barns, and some not so old, but the buildings of our farm past are here to be seen.

Not long ago a letter to the editor of *Country Living Magazine* spoke of the barn as a vanishing landmark. (The magazine had featured a photo essay several months earlier called "American Barns".) The writer related how their beloved barn was damaged in a windstorm, and how there was not enough financial reserve to repair the extensive damage. The barn had to be removed and a pole barn built in its place, because of its cost effectiveness. The letter went on to relate that the barn siding and hand-hewn beams now graced someone's family room, but that an important part of the landscape of their farm was missing. The letter ended with this statement: "Someday there will be barn tours through New England and the Midwest just as there now are covered-bridge tours - a nostalgic trip back in time for tourists."

As you drive around keep your eyes open for these vanishing works of craftsmanship, and get to know their past.

The earliest barns built in Jackson County were of *Gable Roof* construction. They had limestone or field stone foundations. Sometimes the whole bottom level was stone with a wooden building sitting on top. It is still possible to see a stone foundation barn built into a hill. Such construction afforded extra protection from the elements; the livestock could be housed in the lower portion, while the hay was stored up in the drier wooden part of the barn. These early barns can be identified by their gable roof, rectangular form and small size. As time went on and the farm prospered the farmer might build a lean-to on one side for use as a granary or wagon shelter. When a roof line slopes down on one side it is known as a salt box roof. The gable roof has a steep pitch because originally it was thatched, but thatch proved impractical in regions of severe winters and was replaced with planks or shake shingles. The steep pitch, however, was kept.

This type of barn was built between 1840 and 1900.

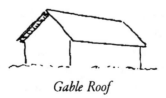

Gable Roof

The barn in the early days of our county was the heart of the farm. When a family finally had enough funds and spare time to put up a barn, they felt they were true farmers and not just sodbusting, stump-grubbing squatters.

Here is an example from 1857 of a threshing.

"There was a large frame barn on our land, part of it was used for a horse stable, part for a granary and corn crib, and in part was what we called a tramping floor, a large room with a double floor where we threshed out the wheat and oats with horses. My father would lay two-courses of sheaves in a circle around the room with the heads overlapping, then a couple of us boys would mount a horse and trot around and around this circle leading another horse, my father continuously turning the sheaves until the grain was all tramped out, after which the straw would be thrown off and the grain run through a fanning mill."

Annals of Jackson County, 1905

After the Civil War the *Gambrel Roof* barn came into favor. This roof gets its name from the shape of a butcher's hook, called a gambrel in French. At this time the barns began to get bigger and longer. Some were very long indeed, housing many work horses or prize cattle.

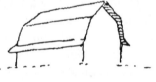

Gambrel Roof, 1860-1920

These early barns were post and beam construction. The wooden joints were pegged; all the vertical members were posts and all horizontal members were beams. Hal Borland, a natural history author, wrote of the old barn on his Connecticut farm as being of post and beam construction. He said it had a framework of hand-hewn beams and round rafters pegged at the peak and adzed flat for the roof boards. The framing was mainly oak and the rafters were white oak. The beams, a good foot square, were mortised together, and the siding was put on vertically.

Barns usually have vertical cladding, up and down boards, often with battens over the spaces between the boards. Battens are wooden or metal slats that are usually thicker in the center to shed water and keep the barns sound. The vertical sheathing harks back to early ship building times, according to Borland, as did most of the early buildings in New England. The vertical boards in barns remain as a feature even if most builders then didn't know of the origin.

Another early type of construction was the *German Barn*. It was similar to the gable roof barn, but had a forebay which hung out over the cattle yard on one side. This forebay gave the animals some protection from the elements. Sometimes it was just a braced roof, other times it was the whole side built out.

German Barn, 1850-1900

A bank barn was built on two levels of ground with a soil bridge leading to the upper level so wagons could be driven onto that floor. Sometimes these were used as threshing floors, too.

The *Three Portal Feeder* barn began to be very popular in the latter decades of the 1800s. It was particularly attractive to the farmers of the Midwest. The use of circular sawn lumber and metal nails as well as more readily available window glass were some of the new features. These barns are lighter and have a rectangular floor plan with gable end doors and a low pitched, or shed, roof. It has a central aisle and enclosed side aisles. The early gable roof and later gambrel roof were expanded to cover the side aisles. Look for the presence of a hay hood and large gable end loft doors.

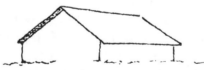

Three Portal Feeder Barn, 1890-1920

Building new barns became less common in the 1920s because the farm economy was suffering hard times. In fact, many Midwestern farmers "lost the farm" during these years. The 1930s were even less stable with the Depression and the added problems caused by the drought. Some non-farm families lived for months on the potatoes they grew, never having the money for luxuries like milk and meat. The Depression hit the Farm Belt nearly as hard as the urban areas, although there weren't as many soup lines. It is said that the bums and drifters knew every soft touch for a handout, and would leave marks on trees and stones to tell other unfortunate, hungry men where a sympathetic farm wife could be persuaded to feed them for an hour's work, chopping wood or hauling water.

The next kind of barn was the *Gothic Barn*. By the 1940s World War II had boosted the food producing economy and barns were being built once more. These barns were used for dairy herds as well as general farm use. The roof was curved or rounded.

71

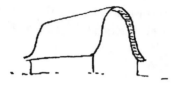

Gothic Barn, 1940s

Other features which give individual barns unique character
are the following:

• **Hay hoods—**
Extensions of gable end of the roof to shelter hay doors.
• **Ventilators—**
Metal ridge structures that were popular in the early 1920s.
• **Door-in-door—**
A human scale door built in a larger wagon door.
• **Dutch door—**
The top and bottom sections of the doors open separately. This allows
for the free flow of ventilation, but keeps animals restricted.

The traditional color of paint for barns has always been red. I've read that this
was the cheapest paint in the 1800s so it was used for farm outbuildings. There are
some classic green barns in Iowa, and white is often the color of dairy barns and
new farm buildings. The most lovely color, perhaps, is the silvery gray sheen with
touches of faded red, almost pink, on an old weathered barn. One winter, we saw
an artist by the side of the road putting the finishing touches on an oil painting of
an old barn, standing off in a snow-covered pasture. As we drove past, what I saw
on the canvas was a barn painted in a shade of yellowish pink over silvery gray.

As you drive by an old barn analyze the shades of gray you see. Be aware also,
that these unpainted boards seem to be in fine shape just under the surface. When
sawed off, the cut edge is a bright yellow, and it smells fresh, like new wood. A
painted or a sided barn is a cared for barn and will be around for our children's
children to see. On the other hand, the lichen on the boards and silvery wooden
shingles create a rich beauty, speaking of decay, but decay enriched with grace.

A farmer did chores in the barn daily, and often those chores were hard work.
There were, however, those sensory rewards: the sight of the misty breath of a work
horse in its stall on a January morning; the soft furry kittens sitting in a shaft of
amber, early morning sunshine coming through a cobwebbed window; the dusty
green smell of a bin of oats; the feel of the hardpacked earth under foot. These
were, perhaps, some compensation to the farmer for the callused hands and sore
muscles. The sights and smells meant good work, enough food, and dignity. The
sights and sounds were the *soul* of the barn.

BARNS TO VIEW

• Limestone Gable: Keiffer Barn, a bank barn. 1850, 243 St. Set back among buildings on north side of road. (See Limestone Loop, Bellevue.)

• Limestone Gable: Gehlen Barn, St. Donatus. West of Gehlen House.

• Salt Box Gable: On Ansel Briggs Highway, Highway 62, outside of Maquoketa. Wooden upper story, limestone foundation and lower story built into hill. (East side of road just beyond trailer park)

• German Forebay: Tabor Farm, on 67 St. Northwest of Baldwin on Jack Tabor farm. Wooden pillars set on stones which support the forebay. Wooden siding, battens. [The Tabor Family Winery is just to the north of this barn.]

• Gambrel Roof: West of Jackson County Fairgrounds, north of entrance road. Land bridge with limestone walls and limestone lower story. Wooden upper story.

• Gambrel Roof: Many along Z15 from Bellevue to Springbrook

• Octagonal Barn: Dyas Farm, viewed from Z15 or 243 St. South of Bellevue

WINDMILLS

The sound of the clanking windmill soothed many a farm child to sleep. Their nostalgic silhouettes remind us of those former farm days. The following is from an article by Lowell Carlson which appeared in the *Bellevue Herald*, March 1984.

The American windmill, dating back to Daniel Halladay's patent in 1854, broke with a thousand year tradition when the young Connecticut mechanic developed a governed windwheel that responded to increasing water pressure from the well. The side vane's horizontal arm caught high winds turning the windmill's wheel to angle with prevailing winds. Counterweights and levers returned the wheel to face the wind when the gust subsided. The wind wheel is set a few inches off-center atop the turntable. As the wind increases the pressure turns the wheel sideways to the force.

SCHOOLS

An 1875 report states there were 147 schoolhouses in the county. Of these, 102 were constructed of wood, thirteen were of brick, eleven were log, and twenty-one were stone. An Iowa ideal: No child would be farther than two miles from a school.

The one-room schoolhouses were often labeled by numbers, but some townships gave their schools names that hint at the natural surroundings of the schools or the names of families in the school district. For example, in Monmouth Township, Section 24, was Watson School, and in Section 35, Tozer School. Mount Pleasant School is in Section 5, and Chattanooga School in Section 12; these may reflect former places of residence for a district family. Pleasant Hill School in Section 10 tells us that the spot where the school was built was on a hill with a pleasing aspect. Or maybe the builders hoped it would be pleasant.

Looking through old platbooks one finds many interesting names for schools.

HOUSES

Early farmhouses can be identified by the roofline in some cases. Look for the angle-back cornice returns of the Greek Revival style, 1830-1870. Often the door is in the long side, and this roofline is in the gable end.

Another clue to the period of architecture is the window treatment. Very small upper story windows called half windows are indicative of 1860s farmhouses. Eyebrow tops or rounded windows were popular in the 1870s.

Lots of gingerbread, technically called bargeboard, and fancy porches with milled woodwork and shadowboards under the gable, were all the rage in the 1880s and 1890s. The numerous sawmills, and the plentiful wood supply made wooden trim affordable, as well as the height of Victorian fashion.

The typical farmhouse of the 1860s to 1880s was in the "L" or "T" shape, the kitchen being in the single-story portion which often had a front and back porch. The parlor was in the downstairs portion of the two-story section, sometimes there was a big window with small, colored glass panes around the edge. This big window often faced north or east to keep the strong sunlight out of the seldom-used parlor and its furniture and rugs.

From 1880 to 1925 the farmhouses became two-story square houses with hip roofs. They were often no nonsense, no frills attached affairs because the majority of farm capital was being spent on huge barns and other outbuildings. I call these "four square" houses.

OUTHOUSES

Once upon a time every house in the county had an outhouse in the backyard, often with a planting of hollyhocks (which are heavy feeders) around it. The outhouses in the country survived for many years after the ones in town were replaced by indoor plumbing. Today there are few outhouses left, and it becomes a game to see if you can spot one or more on any drive. Make a special mark for them on your map!

STREAMS

Play the "map game" with streams, trying to identify even the littlest ones. A detailed map, with the names of streams like Pumpkin Run, is available at the County Engineer's Office at the Court House in Maquoketa. For the smaller streams, an old platbook may be necessary. Here are some interesting names:

- Jess Branch in Sections 13 and 24 of Perry Twp. Feeds into Brush Creek.
- Pinehem Creek in Sections 16 and 9 of Washington Twp. Emptying into a slough north of Green island.
- Scrambling Creek in Sections 31, 36 and 26 of Union Twp. Flows south into Clinton County southwest of Sabula area.
- Pumpkin Run (Also called Punkin Run) in Sections 31, 30, 20 and 17 where it joins the South Fork of the Maquoketa at Joinerville. South Fork Twp.
- Shelley Hollow Creek, in Sections 34, 33 and 28 of Monmouth Twp. It joins Bear Creek.

CHURCHES

Do some "church crawling" (as opposed to "pub-crawling"). Visit ones of different construction, brick, limestone or clapboard. Check out the belltower, and the shape of the windows; are they stained glass?

Here are the names of just a few to start with:
- St. John's Evangelical Lutheran, St. Donatus; brick.
- St. Donatus Catholic Church; stone with stucco.
- Pieta Chapel, St. Donatus, overlooking town; stone.
- Holy Rosary Church, LaMotte, on hill at west edge of town; brick.
- St. Paul's Lutheran, LaMotte, by town square; clapboard.
- St. Patrick's Church, Garryowen; stone.
- Salem Lutheran Church, Andrew; stone.
- Green Island Congregational Church, clapboard.
- United Methodist Church, Sabula, begun in 1853; brick.

OAK SAVANNAS

The remnants of oak savannas to be seen in Jackson County are but a minuscule portion of what must have been here in the 1830s when settlers arrived. Early accounts speak of the parklike groves of trees, with no underbrush. The annual prairie fires kept down the brush and the oaks were unharmed by the flames. The flora survived under the mighty trees' shade as part of a specialized community. In some places, where grazing has not been too intensive, these plants remain in communities, and are both unique and rare.

To recognize an oak savanna remnant look for large oak trees with horizontal limbs, and living uncrowded, each beyond their neighbor's dripline, in a grassland setting. There may be few understory trees and bushes; the feeling is truly one of a park. (Occasionally hickory trees are present, but they also live in their own groves.) Often there will be limestone outcroppings associated with oak savannas, and they may, in fact, be the reason for the savannas which have survived in areas unsuitable for tillage.

- On D55 to La Motte from south of St. Donatus. There are several savannas north of the highway and down draws.
- Highway 61 and 175 St. On northwest corner of the intersection.
- 216 Ave., southern portion of road just before it joins 180 St. Section 34 of Richland, and/or, Section 6 of Perry Township.
- Highway 62 and 92 St.
- Bellevue-Cascade Road, D61, a mile east of Cottonville. Many of the draws have large oak trees.
- E17, a mile west of Springbrook. It looks like the road cut right through this one.
- The area around Rockdale Road and 200 Ave. Rare combination of oak savanna and sand prairie.

Hickory Grove to view:
- Bellevue-Cascade Road, one quarter mile west of Bellevue, north side of the road.

COWS

Cows seem to have the most scenic spots. There they are by a cool, rushing stream, with sweet William blooming along the banks. They graze among the tumbled limestone blocks on steep bluffs and on a sultry afternoon lay down in the shade of mighty oaks. There they chew their cud and doze, watching through long eyelashes as the clouds build in the west. Lucky cows.

SUNRISES

There are a thousand places in Jackson County from which to watch the sun rise. In fact any ridge or bluff with a clear view of the east. But lots of walking to get to them is part of that viewing. I'm proposing places where you can sit in your cozy car, coffee mug steaming and watch the sky. Your car can be like a portable living room. I know this is an indulgence, but it is relatively harmless in comparison with the overall scheme of things in America today; compared to jet vacations, Disney World and gambling casinos, it seems a tiny luxury. So indulge yourself.

Of course, be aware that parking out by a gravel road at the crack of dawn is not considered average (read: "sane") behavior and you will be out of place. Someone may stop to see if you need help. Just smile, say "no", tell them you're waiting for a ride to work. They'll still think you're strange, but at least productive, and go on their way.

The sunrise begins with faint gray light over the horizon. The birds wake up and talk quietly, twittering and calling. Then come the "rosy-colored fingers of dawn"— remember the Odyssey, by Homer?

As the light increases, the surroundings appear. The trees and silos gradually show up, black silhouettes on the horizon. As the whole sky turns an intense yellow, a melted gold shimmer appears on the eastern range. The round sun rises, and can seem to shift shape, sometimes appearing to flow along the rim of the hills. It is incredibly bright!

A sunrise is greatly enhanced by a few clouds. They reflect the glory of the sun before it has begun to peek over the hills, and they fling themselves like gaudy scarves across the sun's face.

Take along a warm blanket to snuggle in, a thermos of a hot beverage, and a book. I would suggest poetry or the Bible or philosophy. Try Tielhard de Chardin (Difficult!), or Hal Borland, Gladys Taber, or Virginia Woolf. These books offer insights that generate reflection, and so you will read for a few minutes, then look up at the sky to see the new vision of quiet splendor, and contemplate the visual beauty and the words you have just read. In a few minutes, after a sip of tea, go back to more reading, then more looking up and so on.

Ah, heaven—to begin each day in such a way would be my idea of heaven on earth.

Places to park to see the sunrise:
- John Henry Weber County Park north of Bellevue off Highway 52. Birch trees across the road.
- On Y61, at the County Home Cemetery entrance road, 189 St.
- Pine Valley Kiosk, east side of 30 Ave. south off E17.
- Dark Hollow Road ridge in Section 11, wide enough shoulder to pull over, one mile south of 81 St.
- Cornelius Seed Corn road off E17, between Springbrook and Andrew.
- Gazebo overlooking Mississippi River, Bellevue River Walk. (You'll have to get out of the car for this one.)

Chapter *6*

Ghost Hamlets I – The Forks

Lost Iowa

Where are the remains of the people buried?
As we drive by, nothing is there but their story.
Where are the remains of the people buried?
Perhaps if we stopped
and shouted out its name
This place would echo back alive again
Streets would show their dusty selves
Buildings would sit straight and firm
on what now seems a lonely stone wall
Could we bring back a young family full of hope
See them at the far edge of the horizon
Just driving down into a greening Spring?
Where are the remains of the people buried?
The echo strikes within each of us
As we look for, and
with each of us
As we listen to
their story.

Charles Jorgensen

THE FORKS

It is good to go in search of former towns. It is good to place oneself on the site of someone's dream town, look around and see nothing but an intersection of two county roads, and the rolling farm land. It's good because it focuses our awareness on what is lasting through many lifetimes. The beauty of nature is timeless, but the works of civilization are temporary and dated in usefulness. Nevertheless, we keep building and searching for the perfect place to live. It is good to be on the site of all the positive, powerful energy necessary to generate these dreams and these towns.

Jackson County has been the inspiration for many hopes and dreams; some flourished, and some never came to be. Some dreams were about getting rich; it was believed that a mill was a surefire way to financial security, and the western part of the county was blessed with abundant water power. Therefore, many mills were built, and many little towns were established at the site of a mill.

The twelve ghost hamlets of this tour are illustrative of the shift from water power of the 1840s through the 1860s, to the railroad service of the 1870s. Nearly all of them were founded near water, a mill being the most important business, and nearly all of them were passed by when the rails were laid in the county. By 1880 most of the towns found their fates sealed, and by 1920 little was left of them. People and businesses had moved to be close to the railroad. When automobiles and rural free mail delivery became a part of farm life throughout the state, the last bit of village independence dried up. It would seem that as individuals got more independence, individual communities lost theirs. The farmers didn't have to depend on the country store for supplies and seed, they could hop in the Model T and—if the roads weren't too muddy—be in Maquoketa, or Bellevue, or Clinton within the hour.

Some believe that the past lives on, replaying over and over, but on a different plane of time than ours. Some also believe that there are doors which can be opened into those other planes of time. I believe that history is the door to the realms of the past. It is possible to know so well the history of a place or era that it is almost like being there.

As you travel to the Ghost Hamlets of Jackson County perhaps you will come to know a kindred feeling, a connection with the settlers who had such high hopes for their fledgling communities. Impressions and stories illustrating the essence of each place, will be joined by some facts. Don't stop to pay too much attention to these tidbits of data; store them away and eventually the view of the past will become more clear. It is like one of those visual puzzles that appear to be nothing but patterns of lines and dots, but as you gaze, trancelike, at the center, suddenly a picture emerges and your perception is deepened and altered. It is possible that a similar experience could be waiting for you in the hamlets. These places and their ghosts can change how you see the past.

In getting to know the ghost hamlets we have a glimpse of the history of early Jackson County. Open the door and walk into the past. Enjoy the trip!

Some of the stories that I will tell you are not exact truth, or at least I don't think they are. You see they came to me. Maybe the ghosts of the hamlets whispered them to me, or maybe the stories are just random bits that were floating around in my imagination. I am sure, whatever the case, that the tales were inspired by the people who once lived here, who died and are buried here; who loved, and worked, and dreamed here. Can you hear their whispers?

THE GHOST HAMLETS I

BUCKHORN

On Highway 64 about five miles west of Maquoketa is the picturesque setting of Buckhorn. With the white steepled church, the cemetery up the hill, the farmhouses, the stone schoolhouse, and the chuckling stream—Buckhorn has all the elements necessary for a charming village.

Buckhorn has many old stories written about it. It was an important stop on the Anamosa Wagon Road, and stagecoaches carrying the mail stopped to water their horses at Burleson's Buckhorn Tavern. The passengers in the coach could get down and come in for a meal. Perhaps there would be fried prairie chicken, mashed turnips with freshly churned butter melting on top, hot corn fritters drizzled with butter and wild grape jelly, and everything washed down with a cold mug of buttermilk fresh from the stone jar that hung down in the dark, cool well.

The tavern was known as The Buckhorn because out in front was a cedar pole that had many antlers nailed to it and stacked around it. Shadrack Burleson had come to the little valley along Pumpkin Run Creek in 1837. By 1850 when the call of the California Gold Rush had thousands of movers on the trail west, he had a very busy hostelry. This tavern, now a residence, stands just west of that creek and to the north of the highway, an example of the building techniques of that day.

> "The house stands as a fit monument to the architects of other days
> who took the rough sawn lumber and hand planed as necessary, made
> by hand all mouldings, rabbet and panel work. Some of the joists in
> the Burleson house were worked out with a whipsaw."
>
> *Annals of Jackson County,* 1906

"Shade", as he was known, was something of a character. He had strong moral beliefs about taking care of his fellow human beings as shown by the assertion that he never turned away anyone with an empty belly simply because they had a flat pocketbook. He spoke up on his political convictions as well, and was an arbitrator in local disputes. Some folks thought the world of him, and some couldn't abide him. But it is said that all, friend and foe alike, respected and even valued his advice.

This story shows an aspect of his character. . .

At this time there were perhaps a score of boys from eight to fourteen years of age in the Buckhorn region and no swimming hole short of the river over a mile from the schoolhouse. Up stream from Mr. Burleson's land there were high banks to the creek and the boys concluded by damming the creek a short order duck could be had at any hour of the day. After a good deal of hard work, carrying stones and cutting rods, a good strong dam was constructed that, when full would afford water neck deep to a mighty good swimming for goslings such as we. For twenty rods down stream in those days Mr. Burleson and others depended upon the stream flow for stock water. When the water failed to come down for a day or such a matter, Mr. Burleson began to think of looking up the source of the drought. He and several who happened to be staying around the tavern, took spades and started for that dam. The water had risen to within several inches of the top and the water looked so inviting, as it was a warm day, that the younger men could not resist taking a plunge before they drained the pond. Mr. Burleson was fond of sport himself and a great athlete and after watching the others a minute or so threw off his clothes and sought the cooling waters, after which the dam was destroyed and thirsty stock below reveled in the waters that came down, from the boys hoped-for swimming hole.

Annals of Jackson County, 1906

The sad part of that story was that the boys had to watch the destruction of their dam from the window of their schoolroom. It was a hot, late spring day, but they never got to swim in that delightfully cool pond.

Once upon a time this picturesque village had a post office, a school, a church and later a co-op creamery down the road. Still later, keeping up with the times, a little filling station appeared across from the church. All this was not enough to keep back the march of time, and the folks who had once stopped for that cool drink and some gossip, moved on.

Facts About Buckhorn (I)

- South Fork Township, Section 29
- First named Waterford, after Waterford, N.Y., the eastern home of many of the early settlers.
- The white clapboard church was built in 1878 by the Reformed Congregation; they had it all paid off with donations by the time it was finished. It's now used as a Community Building.
- The little filling station is gone now, torn down when the highway was widened in 1982, but Patrick Costello painted a nostalgic picture of it and this can be seen at his 'Old Mill Gallery'.
- Buckhorn Creamery began in 1899 and won many awards for butter production and quality. The co-op which went out of business in 1963, was called Farmers Union Cooperative Creamery Company and had customer appreciation picnics which drew thousands.
- Buckhorn Tavern was a hotel, but never a bar, on the Clinton to Anamosa Wagon Road.
- When the railroad came through, Burleson boarded the workers at his own expense. The railroad rewarded his generosity with a life time pass.

NASHVILLE

The town of Nashville probably came into existence because of the railroad. Train tracks were being laid down all across Jackson County in 1872, the year Nashville was platted. Remember that the trains were powered by steam, and needed a big drink of water about every five miles. So little hamlets sprang to life along the locomotive's route to keep it replenished and puffing along.

On the trains came the traveling salesmen. Can't you just imagine a thin young man dressed in a tight, green-plaid suit, burgundy spats, and bright yellow leather boots as he steps down from the train at the depot platform in Nashville?

His face might register contempt for such a tiny place, after all he would be accustomed to the glitter and dash of Clinton! He might think, "Small pickings, but then, maybe not *too* small."

Setting his sample case down he takes the *1890 Rand McNally Shippers' Guide*, a slim volume, from his breast pocket and looks up "Nashville." "Here it is. . . population of 45." He muses, "There are undoubtedly at least twenty ladies in this town just pining for my latest edition of *Madame Leigh's Etiquette and Fashion Book*". As he thinks this he pronounces each vowel in etiquette, making it sound like "*ee tie qwét tee*." Resolved to give Nashville a try he replaces "The Guide" in his pocket, hefts his sample case, heavy with copies of the leather-bound Etiquette, and heads for the American Express Office in the depot to send a telegram. He walks a bit lopsided because of the excessive weight of the case but he still has the sense of style to tip his brown bowler hat over one eye and attempt a saunter.

He has decided to take a later train and will send a telegram on to his usual boardinghouse at Monmouth. It will read, "Hold room stop will take supper stop J.A. Smithersbee."

Checking his change purse, he decides against the telegram. He turns the corner of the depot to head for the first white clapboard house on the block, he hears the soft puffing of the train engine being filled at the stilty watertower by the tracks. He whistles a popular tune; he has high hopes for Madame Leigh's powers of attraction, and his own powers of persuasion. And as he turns up the dirt path to his first potential sale he smiles and thinks to himself, "My, yes, that is apple pie I smell. . . and fresh-brewed coffee. *Mm-mmm.*"

Nashville hasn't been a train stop for many years, but it has loyal homeowners who like its "one-big-neighborhood" friendliness.

FACTS ABOUT NASHVILLE (2)
- South Fork Twp, Section 19
- The town was once known as Pumpkin Center, it sits near Pumpkin Run Creek.
- The railroad was the Chicago and Northwestern and the tracks were taken up in the 1960s.

MILL ROCK

At Mill Rock the southern border of Jackson County is not far away. The country is pleasant here by Bear Creek, with roads curving around the limestone bluffs which shelter the stream. Eden Valley Conservation Park is just a mile away, and is enjoyed year round by picnickers, hikers and nature lovers.

Back in 1836, the Pence brothers might have camped near the Mill Rock site when they came through to map out a road for Mr. Clark, later called the Buffalo Road or Clark's Trail. They would have trudged alongside Bear Creek for a few miles before it swung off to the east, and we can imagine their moccasins splashing through spring-fed brooks, which in turn fed the larger creeks and eventually led to the Maquoketa's South Fork. The land was a vast rolling prairie, but well-watered and with many timbered valleys abundant with deer and elk.

Mill Rock has a remnant community where once a thriving "flouring" mill, as a grist mill was sometimes called, sat on the banks of Bear Creek. The plat shows the streets all laid out, and once there were nearly a hundred people living here.

That thirsty steam engine, however, needed a drink by the time it had huffed and puffed its way from Nashville to Baldwin. And Baldwin, being less rocky, got the tracks and the customer trade.

Soon flour could be bought more cheaply at the store. The supplies were brought in by the locomotive. Sloper's Mill went out of business and in 1916, the limestone school closed down.

The school stood empty by the road, with the zippy Model T automobiles replacing the quieter, plodding horses. The dust settled on the school windows. But the townsfolk had too much community pride to let this good building deteriorate, so a group bought it and turned it into a community center where they celebrated everything from Golden Anniversaries, to the Fourth of July, to Halloween.

By this time it was the 1930s and the Depression was in full swing. Everybody seemed to be cash-poor. (My mother, who grew up during the Depression, quips that she had just three dresses; one hung on a wire hanger ready for church or funerals, another hung on a peg waiting to be ironed, and the third hung on her!)

Times were hard then, nevertheless, people tell stories of the fun to be had for little cost. Mill Rock School was the site of the Saturday night dances. The musicians stood up in the front of the old schoolroom; there might be just a fiddler and a fellow working an accordion. At the door, the men only were charged admission—a quarter, and the ladies were allowed in free. (I suppose they thought that the more women, the more men would show up and pay their two bits.) In they would come; the women dressed in their newest and brightest feed sack dresses. Now in those days material bought on the bolt was too costly, so you went to the feed store where the feed sacks were made of good printed cotton, and for the price of the feed you had some material. If you were lucky you could find enough sacks of the same pattern to make a dress. When it was stitched up, starched, ironed nicely, with its white lawn collar attached, it made a very nice looking outfit. All the women and girls wore them, so it was alright. As long as everyone was poor together it didn't seem to matter so much.

The men wore clean overalls and white shirts that were stiff with the ironed starch. When you got close you could smell the starch, and the rose oil on their still damp, slicked-down hair. Their foreheads were white, but their cheeks and neck were brick red, they had what is called a "farmer's tan".

The gals smelled sweetly of "Sweetheart Soap", a few daring ones might splash on a little "Evening in Paris" or "White Violets." Some carried a hanky sprinkled with cornstarch, to dab at their palms before dancing with their partners. (The men had rubbed liberal amounts of "Bag Balm" or "Cornhusker's Lotion" into their hard, work-callused hands and were kind of slippery to hang on to.)

They danced in pairs, and they danced in squares, and sometimes the women danced together when their old men refused to dance anymore. As all the folks danced, the soft light from the lanterns shone out the windows and up into the big branches of the trees that stood around the school. The music flowed out into the night where the little kids played *"Star Light, Star Bright, first star I see tonight, I wish I may, I wish I might, have the wish I wish tonight."* They played "Statue", and they played "Ghost", a game guaranteed to scare the "bejeesus" out of the youngest ones.

There was a little lunch stand behind a board counter in one corner of the schoolroom, and the smell of hot dogs and coffee joined the odors of kerosene, damp starch, "Evening in Paris", and the cloying and earthy underscent of manure that went along with such country gatherings no matter how hard the shoes were wiped.

My, it *was* fun!

Facts About Mill Rock (3)

- Monmouth Twp. Section 27
- The town was first named Cobb.
- Oldest town in Monmouth Twp., platted in 1854
- Some families from Canada came to the area to settle in the early days.
- The Rand, McNally Shipper's Guide of 1890 shows a population of 78, with mail shipped to Baldwin.
- About the same time that the trains began carrying flour to Baldwin, the 1870s, a wheat blight hit the Midwest, and the bottom went out of the market. Farmers around here never again raised much wheat.

FRANKLIN

North of Baldwin is the site of Franklin, at the intersection of Y34 and 67th Street. A hand-drawn map from an old county record book shows the exact location, Section 10, Monmouth Township.

The Lubben family was in the process of making a very tidy farm just up the road and perhaps they were interested in encouraging more families to move to the area, so they platted a town and named it Franklin.

I don't know how the process of registering a plat works, but it would have been necessary to record it at the county courthouse. In 1859 the county seat was in Bellevue, clear across the county on the banks of the Mississippi.

The plat was taken out by Henry Lubben on December 16, 1859. He and his wife, Elizabeth, signed it and ". . .acknowledged the opening of the streets for public use as therein set forth to be in accordance with their desire and to be their voluntary act and deed. This approval of the survey and placement of permanent stakes at all the corners of all the lots and stones of the dimension prescribed by law were placed at some point of every street. Given by J. Kelso, County Judge."

The interesting handwritten document about the plat shows the streets: Franklin Street running east and west, and State Street, running north and south, about where Y34 is now. The plat was recorded by R.B. Wyckoff, a man whose name pops up in early records of the county. He appears to have been an educated man and an able politician.

I am imagining the 16th of December in the year 1859. The Lubbens, Henry and Elizabeth and their children, would have gotten up before first light— long before light, to do the chores. Chores included drawing water from the well or the spring, for the house and the barn; feeding and watering the cow, the sheep, and the oxen; milking the cow; bringing in wood and building up the fire to fix breakfast and to heat the stones for the journey. When breakfast was eaten and all the chores done, the oxen were yoked and the sled trace attached. The sled had a large wooden box filled with hay, maybe it was prairie hay. Everyone had bundled up in their warmest clothes; all woven and sewn by Elizabeth. The hot stones were put into the sled and the children were nested in the hay and a buffalo robe put over them. Mother and father had another robe draped around them where they sat on three-legged milking stools at the front of the box. Their feet were on hot stones and the straw was packed in around their legs. The runners had been planed smooth by a hand adze and they cut through the snow cleanly as the oxen walked along much more quickly than we might imagine.

The distance from Baldwin to Bellevue is twenty to twenty-five miles across country. If it had been very cold the river and the streams would be frozen and more easily crossed, and in that day it was easy to pass through the timbered land because the annual prairie fires kept down the understory growth and brush. The woodlands were like well-tended groves.

Can oxen make four miles an hour? At whatever rate they traveled it is sure that the family was hungry when they arrived at Bellevue, and ready for the lunch Elizabeth had packed. She had included a crock of soft cheese, buckwheat cakes, and crunchy apples from the attic barrel. They drank cold milk from a crock.

At the courthouse the paper was signed, the legal process completed, and then, perhaps, the family visited the store. Only a few coins were needed to get the children pieces of hard candy and Elizabeth thread and needles. While they did their shopping, the stones could be heated up at the stove to be put back into the sled for the journey home.

The early evening darkness came down quickly and the children soon fell asleep, snuggled and warm, and a little sticky from their candy. Henry talked quietly to the oxen, encouraging them on home to the warm barn and their manger of hay.

The stars were shining brightly on the glistening snow when the sleepy family got back to their sturdy limestone farmhouse. That night they dreamed of the new town of Franklin and of all the people who would move to it. But alas, hardly anyone ever did.

FACTS ABOUT FRANKLIN (4)

- Platted in 1859, Monmouth Twp., Section 10
- The fine limestone structures in the region are representative of the heritage of European immigrants and of the German settlers from Pennsylvania.
- Henry Lubben came from Germany in 1834.
- John Lubben, descendant of Henry Lubben, is present owner of the land where Franklin was platted, and resident just up the road.
- Was the town named after Benjamin Franklin? (That's a question, not a fact. . . sorry.)
- In fairness to the facts, it is possible that Henry and Elizabeth merely signed a paper notarized by their neighbor, J.K. Hershberger, on December 16th. It is possible that it was recorded later in Bellevue. But I like my imagined story too much to support this more realistic explanation wholeheartedly. So I support it halfheartedly.

EMELINE

It is interesting that Emeline was once known as "The Four Corners" because that is about all that's there today. There are some houses, and there's the former schoolhouse to the south which is maintained by all the 4-H and Saddle clubs that use it. It was purchased by the Brandon Township Trustees from the schoolboard in the 1960s for one dollar. And now, just as when classes were held in the school, it is the heart of the community.

Once there was a church on the northwest of the four corners. But folks moved away, or went to bigger congregations in town, or just passed away, and it was abandoned in the early 1980s and is gone now.

Once there was a blacksmith shop, but it burned down, and there was a cream station but it closed. There was a doctor's office, but, well, you know, it's gone, too.

When visiting with folks about Emeline, one thing always comes up, and that is the General Store. They say things like, "Now that was an example of everyone's idea of a country store." Or they might say, "The west wall was just covered with old pictures and such—from doings around here—it was like a local museum." Some folks also mention the "drop of rain."

I can imagine two old timers and a young boy sitting on a bench out in front of the store, under the tin awning. It is the turn of the century and they are dressed in overalls and straw hats. It is raining gently and one old timer says to the boy, "Sonny, you know, when a drop of rainwater falls on that road there, halfa' that drop flows off to the north over there (he gestures with his pipe) and halfa' that drop flows down to the south (again pointing with his pipestem). The halfa' that drop that trickles north joins up with lots and lots of other little drops and they run downhill and wiggle past rocks until they finally slip into the *North* Fork of the Maquoketa. But now that little halfa' drop of rainwater that headed south, it runs and runs until it finally flows right into the *South* Fork of the Maquoketa. Why that road out there, (pointing again) that road is like what you might call the County Divide. Yes sir, the County Divide, not the Continental Divide. You have heard of the Continental Divide, haven't you, boy?"

"Yes, sir." the boy says.

"Good," the old timer says and nods his head, "I'm glad that teacher marm is teaching hard things to you younguns'. It's good to know that hard stuff about places far away, like the mountains out in the West. But, I'm teaching you something too, about right here, right where we sit. This is the highest spot anywhere abouts and it is right smack dab between the North Fork and the South Fork. So when a drop of rain falls it just naturally has to break in half, and half of it goes north and half of it goes south. What you think, boy? Do you think that's so?"

"Yes, sir."

"Well, you're right, it *is* so! And don't you go and forget it now. It's important to know things about home, too."

"Yes, sir."

The old timer turns to his crony and says, "Well, let's go into the store and get a cup of coffee. I'm all tired out from all that educating I been doing. We'll just let this boy think on that hard lesson he's been learning."

After they had gone into the store the boy sat awhile, watching the rain. Then he jumped down from the porch, hunching his shoulders up against the rain and splashed his barefoot way through the puddles to the dirt road in front of the store. There he hunkered down to watch a single rain drop divide itself, and watched to see half of it flow north, and half of it flow south. From the window the old timers watched him and chuckled softly.

The Emeline Country Store burned down in the 1960s. None of the memorabilia could be saved, but the story about the drop of rain lives on.

Facts About Emeline (5)

- Emeline is in Brandon Twp. in Section 22
- The Country Store was on the ridge road that is now E17.
- It had a post office as early as 1854 and was in operation until 1900.
- Also known as Wagonersburg.
- It is said to have had the first dial telephone system in the county.
- Look at a map and see the ridge road and the creeks flowing away on either side of the ridge.

CANTON

If you stop into the Longbranch Tavern and Cafe in Canton, you might notice an old photograph of the mill that once stood just north of the bridge. The picture hangs over the counter and shows little tykes by the mill; their clothing puts the time at about the turn of the century. The mill appears to have been clapboard, and several stories high with some windows. There was a mill race or pond, too. In the background are several houses neatly painted and with fancy wooden porches.

The village of Canton was once so forthcoming, it was called a city in the *Plat Book and Atlas of Jackson County*, 1913. But, truthfully, I believe that quote to have been from a much earlier time. The *city* plat had thirty blocks, half on the east side of the river, wedged in under a bluff. There was even an East Canton just north of the present E17 on the east side of the river.

Why was this place once called a city and so prosperous? Well, the mills were important, and for many years the business of making barrels kept many men employed.

"Away back in the early fifties, when the territory lying between the north and south branches of the Maquoketa was covered with a dense growth of Primeval forest, the chief industry of the country was coopering, and almost every settler was engaged in that business. The timber consisted largely of oak. The red oak timber converted into flour barrels, and the white oak into whiskey barrels, and pork barrels, and the principal market for this product was Galena."

History of Jackson County, 1879

One old source says that in 1850 there were 1,200 residents in Canton, rivaling Dubuque in size. Even accounting for some exaggerating, that seems a bit high, but the little town was certainly more lively then, than it is now.

It is said that Kelsall's Stone Store was a beautiful building. It was in operation until around 1940, when it burned down. The building housed a post office, a pool hall, and a hotel. It sat halfway up the rise from the river and south of the highway; the foundation stones are still visible.

Closer to the river is the stone school and just south of it is where the old bridge once crossed the river.

Life in old Canton, for a young man, was idyllic. Every morning when the sun came up over the bluffs the river sparkled and it ran fast and clear. There was good fishing in that river. All the boys ran a trotline overnight, and checked it every morning. Many families had fried catfish for lunch, firm and sweet-tasting under its cornmeal coating.

In the fall, a fella' could take his .22 and his dog, and hunt squirrels in the oak groves up on the bluffs. Rabbits were good hunting in the winter when the snow fell.

There were chores to be done at home, of course, before a fella' could take off to go hunting. Chores like chopping wood, or bringing in a bucket of cobs for the cob-burning range, or filling the reservoir on the stove on wash day with water pumped from the cistern. In the garden the rows of green beans required lots of hoeing and the potatoes needed hilling up.

It was always a good idea to earn some spending money, too, and there were plenty of odd-jobs to be done around town. One young man used his accumulated wealth to buy "shorts", a cheaper kind of cartridge for his .22 rifle. Grandma Mabel would give a nickel tó have all the windows washed and the rugs beaten. The poolrooms needed to be swept out most days; that was good for a penny. Stocking shelves at the store and sweeping the loading platform would pay a penny.

Nearly every summer's afternoon there would be a ball game down by the school with little kids and older boys and girls all taking their turns at bat, and their turns at chasing down the ball in the poison ivy patch in the woodlot. When too hot and too dusty to play anymore, the river was there waiting to be plunged into. They would jump in and paddle around, and then crawl up on the bank and dry off in the late afternoon sun.

Life was good. An idyllic life indeed.

FACTS ABOUT CANTON (6)

- In Brandon Township, Section 19
- The "city" was platted in 1855
- It was once hoped that the railroad would come through Canton, it never did.
- It was once hoped that a hydroelectric dam would be built at Canton, but the bottom of the river wasn't right for it.
- It was once hoped that a gold rush would center on Canton as gold was found in Black Hawk Creek east of town. It never did.
- A post office was established in 1846 and discontinued in 1919.
- Remember one old source said that 1,200 residents lived in Canton in 1855? Another source said that the number of residents in 1855 was 150. History! What can I say? Take your pick!
- Once there was a grist mill, a sawmill, a woolen mill, a packing house, a coopering trade, 2 doctors, 6 thriving stores, smithies and wagon shops, a few tavern/poolrooms and a school.

OZARK

Ozark is surrounded by the rough and timbered terrain found along the North Fork of the Maquoketa River. It once had a woolen mill and a grist mill and quite a few inhabitants, but now instead of signifying the name of a town, "Ozark", stands for the name of an area. The limestone bluffs which border the North Fork are found here in a continuous parade. And the trees are like the crowds of onlookers watching from the sides of the swiftly flowing, and sometimes rocky stream. The stream seems gently musical, and sounds like a band of woodwind instruments—all marching along on tiptoe. But in early spring, when the ice goes out, it seems more like a rowdy circus parade with trumpeting elephants and roaring lions; like the sounds of the iceflows breaking up—with much tearing and grinding.

The area was first "improved", an old account says, in 1848. By 1850 there were five slab shanties. A slab shanty is built of roughsawn planks of wood set on end in a trench dug in the ground instead of a sill of wood being set on a foundation. The walls were double, the slabs placed face to face and solidly nailed together, which left the walls as rough on the inside as on the outside This would make a strong, warm house, one story high, with a slab-covered roof. I can't help but wonder if these were mainly "baching" cabins. I hope there weren't too many women who had to make a home out of a dark and airless slab shanty, no matter how warm and snug it was! The men working in the mills wouldn't care much about such fancies as windows with the light and fresh air they let in, for when they got back from work it would be dark anyway and they had all the fresh air they needed during the day. So once again, let me say, I hope these were "baching" cabins.

I have visited with a woman who lived at Ozark all the years of her married life. She raised her family there, and she helped burn the native grasses so that the cattle had new green grass to eat each spring. As a result, much native prairie habitat was preserved here. She walked these bluffs and fished in the stream. On hot summer afternoons, she and her little sons would walk upstream to a sandy beach shaded by the trees high up on the bluff. The boys would play in the sand and she would sit on a kitchen chair she had lugged along. The breeze off the cool water was refreshing and before they went home to fix supper they would have a little wade near the edge of the beach.

Sometimes, she and her husband, would go fishing in the river, but they didn't always take fishing poles. Sometimes, they fished by catching the catfish with their hands! As I understand it, the catfish doze in holes in the bank, so you stick your hand into a hole and catch the drowsing catfish! It sounds awful, and fear-inspiring to me. One time her husband caught a big fish that took his hand and swallowed it up to the forearm. Who caught whom? The Ozark fisherfolk are tough!

How special to have had this whole wild river valley as one's backyard.

The Ozark Wildlife Area is down a road to the east and at the base of the bluffs. Those bluffs are hidden in summer by the lush growth of understory trees, such as the grey dogwood and honeysuckle. The grapevines, as thick as a man's arm, drape themselves all through the understory and up into the branches of the trees which tower overhead. The edge of the road is ruffled with jewelweed whose orange blossoms hang like baubles on slender strands; they bounce at the slightest breeze. On the right side of the road is a sandy cornfield and beyond it is the river. On the bluff side it would seem that there are enough rock shelter sites to keep a team of archaeologists busy for years. About a mile along this 'B' level road it begins to rise up onto the rocks of the bluff. Sheer rock is on the left and a sheer drop to the river is on the right. A few blessed trees grow on the right side, between the road and the river. These trees make one feel slightly more secure, but the thought of a possible washout sends tremors into the faint-of-heart. (Me, in this case.)

Those people who drive four-wheel drive "monster" pickups or jeeps seem drawn to 'B' level roads. It is said that after a good rain they partake in an activity called "mudding". Ever notice those vehicles on the streets or roads completely *frosted* in gobs of mud? It drips from the door handles, it's even on the very top of the very tall cab. One can only imagine the kind of driving necessary for that much mud draping. Here, on this road, one encounters the deep ruts that I suspect have been caused by the mudrunners. The ruts are on a curve and up a hill, appearing all at once. They are deeper than the car's undercarriage. The choice is between trying to turn around and risk scraping off the muffler and other assorted parts under the car, or just backing down the shallower ruts and only risk a slide into the river—after a considerable drop. We stopped the car, perched on two ridges between the ruts, and got out to survey the choices. Finally we decided to risk the muffler and a noisy ride back home rather than risk a wet swim to the nearest place to climb out of this cold river! "Experienced" advice from us says to tackle this road by getting out of the car and walking, back where it starts to rise up that bluff face!

No matter the condition of the road, I'm grateful for its solitude. It seems as wild here today as it must have been before either the slab shanties or the mills came into existence. It might have been a good place for a hamlet; but it is a better place to see the river, the bluffs, and the trees; set in place by the hands of the Creator.

FACTS ABOUT OZARK (7)

- In Brandon Township, Section 5, platted in 1848
- A post office was established in 1854
- An 1870 plat shows the town just northeast of the bridge.
- Joseph Hildreth, the founder, wanted to call the town Osage, but postal authorities asked for another name as there was already an Osage in Iowa. So he kept the "O", dumped the "sage" and added a pinch of "zark".
- The Rand McNally Shipper's Guide cites a population of 116 in 1890.
- Ozark Wildlife Area is on 187th Street and is fenced off at the top of a rutted bend!

CRABBTOWN

The North Fork proceeds from Ozark southeastward through bluffs and valleys for about five miles before it comes to the place where Crabbtown once was.

The name of the town did not come from the founder's favorite seafood dish back home on Chesapeake Bay, nor did it come from his feelings regarding his mother-in-law, it came from the brothers Crabb, Isaiah and Washington, who bought the sawmill in 1859, and named the town after themselves.

The name, however, did seem to be a perplexing point over the years, for the town has been known as: Crabbtown, Crabb's Mill, Crabb Hill or just plain Crabb.

A Doctor Blackburn first came and settled the area. He was from Licking County, Ohio, and many of the early settlers came from the same place "Back East". Those settlers' names are many of the same names appearing today on the lists of inhabitants of the region, even in the township of Brandon itself. That is an interesting thing to think about.

Settlers have been moving west since The West first opened up at the end of the Revolutionary War. A family would homestead, fell trees and raise a cabin, break ground for crops, maybe stay for five years, and then something would call them on—like it called the settlers from Licking County, Ohio, to come on to Crabbtown, Iowa. And they would pick up and move, leaving only the graves of their old and of their babies as the markers of their life in that place.

Moving west was exciting for the menfolk. It meant the prospect of a new beginning, fresh horizons, good hunting and the opportunity to make a better life, and maybe even a fortune.

For women, it was all pretty much the same wherever they lived. When they got to the new place the work was just about the same as before, only harder to begin with. A woman had to haul water up from the creek, or from a spring if she was lucky, fix meals at an open fire, dress game, dress the family by making most of their clothes— from spinning to weaving to sewing, bake bread, make a garden, smoke meat, salt-down pork, feed the chickens, milk the cow, keep the toddler from tumbling into the open fire, help at butchering and at harvest, and give birth to the new baby. The scenery might be prettier, but the work was the same. And it was hard to leave family and the friends of youth; it was hard to leave the graves of loved ones.

Nevertheless, for some reason, the people from Licking County, Ohio, came here and liked this part of the West enough to settle and stay. The farms they developed made them a living and life was good enough to stop looking beyond the horizon for something better.

No matter where they lived, work and loneliness seemed to be the pattern of the pioneer woman's life. She stayed home to tend the claim while her man walked to the settlement miles away to record it. She stayed home when he went for supplies. She stayed home while her man went hunting, or went all the way Back East to fetch his parents. Mostly a pioneer woman stayed home all the time. Days or weeks could go by without a visitor, or a reason to put on a clean apron. When churches and schools began to come into a settlement the women were the biggest supporters because they suddenly had folks to visit with, and a good excuse to leave the home place for a few hours.

The women were not all saints, however. They could be shrewish or bitter to the point of never speaking a kind word. They had made uncommon sacrifices to come out West and some never got over it. To give up everything they had known, to move in a wagon and be plunked down in a sparsely inhabited land, a wilderness; that was hard. To have just one pair of decent shoes and to go barefoot all the time to save them; that was hard. To be pregnant and know there wasn't another woman within miles to help at the birthing; that was hard. To be nursing

95

a newborn and not have enough good food to eat to keep body and soul together; that was hard. These things were hard, but were the common lot of women who came into Jackson County before Iowa was a state.

Pioneer women were sturdy, or they died. They were resourceful, or they went without. They were good and loving, or there was no love at all in their little log cabins. Their creed was "love, work, and adapt!"

The early pioneers were hardy and we should feel admiration for their courage and their ability to make a community out of a lawless land. The women did their share even though we rarely read about them or their contributions. So when a quote like the following turns up it makes me feel proud.

> "The story goes that during the War of the Rebellion (The Civil War) so many young men signed up as soldiers that they left the country very short of hands to farm and run the businesses. But around Crabb Mills this difficulty was soon, as least partially overcome. The ladies now began to enlist, not as gunners but as plowmen, as drivers on mowers and reapers, as cornhuskers; in short, they took to themselves all the rights that the men had or could have, except the right to vote at the elections. It is but due to the ladies to here say that to them belongs a full share of credit and honor for the part they took in sharing the burdens, not in the fields of blood but in the harvest fields and other industries that furnished supplies for the vast armies that were battling for the supremacy of the flag of our beloved country."
>
> *History of Jackson County*, Ellis

It is my considered opinion that women had been doing some of those chores right along, but it took a war for the men to notice enough to comment on it. The women, according to diaries of the time, gloried in men's work because they could manage it the way they thought it should be done. And they loved to be able to get out of those long, heavy and encumbering skirts, put on a pair of their husband's or son's pants, and go out into the field to work and not shock the prudish men by such unladylike behavior.

The descendants of those early pioneer mothers live in Jackson County today. The women of the 1990s are still hard workers. They raise a family, have an eight-hour-a-day job outside the home, they chore, help at harvest, volunteer at church and at the school, are good companions, and they love their mates. Women today aren't saints either, but they have learned to follow the creed: "Love, Work, and Adapt!"

Facts About Crabbtown (8)

- In Brandon Township, Section 14
- Post office established in 1879
- The place where the bridge crosses the river was known as Dodge's Ford in the early days. It was such an important spot that two prominent automobile manufacturers named their vehicles after it. (Just kidding about that last sentence. Sorry.)
- Remember that Iowa became a state in 1846 and those early settlers came in 1836! Ten years before laws, schools and in some cases—neighbors.
- Here's an old joke: "How do you keep the old lady at home?" Answer: "You keep her pregnant in summer, and barefoot in winter!" It doesn't seem very far from the reality of a frontier woman's life, and therefore not funny.
- The women who took over the farms or the businesses during war time literally "wore the pants in the family". That saying has come to have a connotation of a henpecked husband, but it's origin might lie in wartime necessity. The problem for men came when they returned home and had to wrest control away from the often very capable women.

IRON HILL

Which of several interesting stories should we explore? We might think about the vigilante hanging of a murderer in 1857. Or about the Iron Hill Community Church and all its activities, or how about my RAGBRAI story? Choices, choices.

Oh well, let's do all three, starting with the sensational, violent, and fit-for-the-tabloids story.

Iron Hill, in its time, was just as much a part of the Wild West as Dodge City, Kansas, or Tombstone, Arizona, were to become. For a period of twenty years or so, from 1838 to 1860, Iowa was on the leading western edge of settlement. The type of personalities attracted to a new country included both the law-abiding, who wished to build up strong communities, and the lawless, who saw an opportunity to take advantage of the lack of social infrastructure. There were horse thieves, counterfeiters, and men known as "bad actors" who looked for a chance to prey on weaker folk. Some felt the law couldn't keep up with the demand for action to keep communities safe. And so the vigilante movement thrived on the frontier.

A vigilante fellowship known as "The Regulars of Iron Hill" grew in size to over 400 men. In 1857 they got stirred up, went to the county jail in Andrew and broke down the door of the jail with sledgehammers. The mob took out a prisoner named Alexander Grifford who was awaiting trial for the murder of another Iron Hill young man. Grifford was marched to a nearby, crooked old oak tree, a noose placed around his neck and he was strung up by strong arms, held dangling for a minute and let down again. He was told that if he would confess he would be put back in the jail to await the judge and jury. He confessed; but the mob mentality was too strong, and they broke their word and they hung him, this time until he was dead.

Hard times on the frontier!

I don't know if the Regulars existed side by side with the religious community who formed a church in 1869, "for the purpose of erecting a church for all denominations to worship the Almighty God". But it is pleasant to think that the church still exists today and has been the inspiration for much good in its many years.

The East Iron Hills Community Church sits on the eastern outskirts of Iron Hill. It is looking very spiffy these days and is the center of a farm community's activities as well as the church home for many families.

The tradition of a church-centered social life was always a part of the farming community and of this part of eastern Iowa. According to the church's recent cookbook of 1996 it has been a focal point for gatherings for years. . ."Camp meetings sometimes lasted a week, Gospel meetings, revivals, choir practice, lectures, ice cream socials and Iron Hill Orchestra musicals were held at the church."

The Iron Hill Orchestra intrigues me. I can imagine a diverse assemblage of musical instruments; a few violins, several mandolins, a piano, clarinet, and a drum or two. Now, I'm just guessing and haven't a shred of evidence to go on. But I am sure that whatever the makeup of the orchestra, the music they made was appreciated. If it was classical music there were perhaps a few who relaxed so much that the sounds of gentle snoring from the audience accompanied the instruments. And if the music was more snappy, there would have been a few comments about such good dancing music going to waste in a church!

Musicians all over the world and throughout time have one thing in common—they love to perform their music. And if the community is not always sure just how to feel about them, whether to be in awe of their special ability, or to be resentful *because* of that special ability, it doesn't stop musicians from making music. So Iron Hill Orchestra, hurrah! I wish I could have heard you play your music.

And now my RAGBRAI story.

Several years back the Des Moines "Register's Annual Great Bike Ride Across Iowa", was going to go through the hamlet of Iron Hill. I was working at a church food stand set up near the intersection of E17 and the Bernard Road. That day the words "iron hill" took on new meaning.

The cyclists would stagger over to our stand and leaning on the counter say, "Tell me about this *Iron Hill*". They emphasized the word "iron" only slightly more than the word "hill". There was a worried look on their faces and a dread in their inflection which we didn't understand at first, knowing only that Iron Hill was a little town just down the road. Then we caught the implication of the name and realized that they feared another big hill after a day's ride of so many hills. When we said it was just the name of the little town, they suddenly stood straighter to ask, "No hill?". When we replied, "No, not really.", they absolutely towered and began to swagger. (We didn't tell them the bad news, about the real iron hill east of Andrew. I must confess that there was one very haughty and rude man whom we didn't relieve of his dread. He needed a little air let out of his tires, so to speak, and we knew he would remember us when he finally got to the iron hill.)

Regulars, Church and Orchestra and an *Iron Hill*; some stories to ponder as you drive along. Let them be an inspiration to good conversation and memories of your own.

FACTS ABOUT IRON HILL (9)

- Farmers Creek Township, Section 29
- An old map shows East Iron Hill, West Iron Hill and Iron Hills all clustered near the present village. The recent cookbook published by the church refers to East Iron Hills Church.
- Post office established 1851, platted 1859.
- General Store building is still standing, but unoccupied.
- East Iron Hills Ladies Aid group serves a baked chicken dinner fundraiser in the new church basement every month. Homegrown food, homemade pie!
- This Ghost Hamlet at one time had: its own telephone exchange, sawmills, cold-storage plant, cream station, stores and two doctors.
- The name for the town might have come from the many iron ore deposits found in the region. There were great hopes in the early days for Jackson County to be an industrial center because of the many mineral deposits.

FULTON

Fulton is a small residential hamlet with the North Fork bending around it from the west and along the south. Of all the towns started on the river it had the best chance of success because it had the room to spread out. At one time it was a prosperous place with mills and with general stores, a doctor and all the accoutrements of village life. But the railroad didn't lay tracks near it and that doomed its hopes of continued growth.

One thing that struck me about Fulton as I looked at old plat maps and read the old stories, were the references to all the churches in this little hamlet. Four different denominations have had churches in Fulton, but not all at the same time it turns out. In fact, one would take over the building when another discontinued services.

Church going was an important aspect of, and was in fact often the reason for, living in or near a village. It was a satisfying thing to have a minister nearby to set a good example for the children. (And the menfolk!)

The two Sunday services and the prayer meeting after choir practice on Wednesday evening gave a purpose to the lives of the members. A good deal of visiting took place around the edges of worship, and was something everyone enjoyed. If the Ladies' Aid Society was coming to your house in May, in April the house would get a good turning-out, to be spring cleaned from attic to cellar. Church kept housewives on their toes.

In the summer there was always a Sunday School Picnic attended by the whole congregation. Here in Fulton, it might have been held west of town on a high rolling bluff above the riverbend. It was a special place with massive oak trees dotting the pasture and large limestone outcroppings with gooseberry bushes at their feet. The slopes of a deep draw leading down to the bottom land were covered in wildflowers like the unusual Indian paintbrush and the crowded umbrellas of the Mayapples. The rocky bluff face and ledges became a mass of blue blossoms when the bluebells came out in May.

Leading up to the bluff top was a sandy hill, a perfect place for kids to tumble and roll down, then run to the river and jump in to get the sand off sweaty skin and out of tangled hair. But this kind of wild behavior was frowned upon at the Sunday School Picnic. Instead, there were sedate, organized games for the children, while the grown ups set up the plank and saw horse tables on the only level ground, by the pasture gate. Tablecloths covered the rough planks and each family spread quilts or blankets on the cropped grass under the oaks. Here they sat to eat the heaped plates of cold fried chicken, potato salad, sour pickles, raised dinner rolls with home-churned butter, chocolate cake iced with cooked vanilla frosting, and lemonade or coffee. A small fire by the gate kept the hanging coffee pot hot all afternoon.

After everyone was too full to eat another bite, the women would put the food away in baskets and deep buckets, and the men would stretch out on the quilts in the shade. They were supposed to keep an eye on the baby, but soon they would cover their faces with their hats, cross their ankles, and with hands on their chests, they would have a short snooze. The women came and sat beside them, perhaps rocking the toddler to sleep.

Older children explored some shallow caves nearby and the oldsters—grandmas and grandpas of those more energetic youngsters—dozed in chairs brought along for them. The horses, tied to the fence, would sleepily swish their tails to keep the flies from biting, all the while chewing oats in their feedbag. All was quiet for a time, only the distant shouts of the children floated back through the tall trees.

As the sun moved west across the sky and the afternoon wore on the blankets would be moved to new patches of shade. The men and children might take a walk to look at the river, while the women just enjoyed sitting and talking quietly among themselves so as not to wake the babies sleeping on their laps.

The period of rest ended all too soon. Children were collected and brushed down and made to sit on the quilt and listen. It being a Sunday School picnic, the minister often preached an *al fresco* sermon. The dappled sunlight lay across his black suit and smooth hair, and the birds twittered in thoughtful "amens". The choir might be talked into favoring the assembled with a few old hymns such as "Rock of Ages" or "Jerusalem, My Happy Home", sung to the accompaniment of a squeeze-box accordion. The congregation would join in on "The Old Rugged Cross" and "Blessed Be the Tie That Binds". The singing sounded so different out of doors. The notes were often blown away by a June gust that tossed the leaves and the women's bonnets.

After the singing, the children would stand up by the minister to say the "pieces" they had memorized in Sunday School class since Christmas. The littlest would have learned the Lord's Prayer and would recite it together with timely prompting from their teacher. Older children could recite The Twenty-third Psalm: "*The Lord is My Shepherd, I Shall Not Want*". Parents beamed with pride at their children's accomplishments.

Ice cream became a part of the picnics in later years. The assembled would share one last dessert of angel food cake or rhubarb pie topped with the soft, frozen custard; yellow, sweet, icy and so refreshing.

The young men would have taken turns hand-cranking the ice cream freezer, thus taking the opportunity to impress the young women with their strength. Mischievous little boys would steal pieces of ice to suck on or to throw at the lovesick older brothers standing around waiting their turns at the crank.

As the late afternoon sun streamed across the pasture, and the folks washed down their pie and ice cream with the last cup of coffee, which always tasted so good at church gatherings, the picnic would come to an end. Good-byes were spoken, recipes exchanged and the horses hitched up—time to head home to do chores.

```
┌─────────────────────────────────────────────────────────────┐
│                  FACTS ABOUT FULTON (10)                      │
│  • In Farmer's Creek Township, Section 23                     │
│  • Platted in 1851                                            │
│  • At one time there were three general stores, several       │
│    blacksmith shops and a Dr. Eckles, and in later years a    │
│    gas station.                                               │
│  • Four churches: Presbyterian, became Methodist; Baptist     │
│    became RLDS. (That building is now a private residence.)   │
│  • In 1852 the town put in a bid to be the county seat, but   │
│    they were unfairly "beat out" according to one old timer   │
│    quoted in an old history.                                  │
│  • Recently the old Presbyterian/Methodist Church, now the    │
│    Fulton Community Church, was set to be either moved or     │
│    demolished because of the construction of the new four-    │
│    lane highway. Time grew short and no interested parties    │
│    came forward to help move the church out of harm's way.    │
│    But at the last moment, funds were accumulated and the     │
│    church was moved back from the highway several blocks.     │
│    Volunteer labor has now added a basement with a kitchen    │
│    and restrooms and it is an even better community center.   │
│    Congratulations Fulton Community Church and all the        │
│    volunteers who worked to save it. There is lots of life    │
│    yet in these tiny towns.                                   │
│  • "Rock of Ages", by T. Hastings, was written in 1830.       │
└─────────────────────────────────────────────────────────────┘
```

HURSTVILLE

The place called Hurstville was a company town. There was once a company store; there were little houses for the workers, and a special branch of the railroad. It was a community which existed to facilitate the business ventures of Alfred Hurst. His "North Side White Lime Kilns" were known all over the United States and the lime was shipped to every corner of this country.

The burning of raw chunks of limestone in intense heat produces lime, and the process requires enormous amounts of timber to keep the fires going around the clock. The region known as the "Big Woods" lying between the north and south branches of the Maquoketa River was ideal for making lime. There were vast stands of timber and easily accessible limestone.

The kilns operated for nearly sixty years, burning limestone in the huge chimneys, with the fires roaring night and day. It is said that eight cords of wood were needed per day for each of the four kilns! The Big Woods lost much of its timber in those years. The lime was shipped in oak barrels made on the site by coopers. Blacksmiths kept the horses shod and the heavy wagons rolling. Other men worked hard felling trees, stoking fires, quarrying limestone, driving the big wagons, and loading the finished product onto wagons and, later, onto the rail cars.

Hurstville Lime Kilns' heyday lasted from 1871 to 1930 when Portland Cement completely took over the mortar market. When the Kilns finally stood quiet, the last fire burned down to cooling ashes, the company town went into a sleepy, half-awake doze that lasted many years. The rather rickety little company houses were homes for folks until the 1980s, when they were torn down. The company store became a tavern/restaurant famed for its tacos, but it too was demolished after extensive damage caused by the floods of 1993. It would seem that the *second life* of the town was over.

You see we don't know much about the *first life* of the inhabitants of the area, the native people. The first dwellers were Indian, although there may not have been a village established here, there was a burial ground well-known by early settlers, and there were mounds to the west of the ridge that were probably territorial markers built by the Woodland Indians. It was a sacred place of reverence for their ancestors.

It is said that north of Sand Ridge, as early settlers referred to it, was an Indian dancefloor. It was hard-packed clay, very smooth and level, and shaped in a large circle. Around the outside edge of the floor were concentric rings of planted cedar trees, making an enclosure where the rhythm of the drums reverberated with throbbing power. By the time Hurst started his lime kilns it had been plowed up for a cornfield.

Think of the contrast between the Sand Ridge Indian village and the Hurstville Lime Kilns, the differences are dramatic. Contemplate the attitudes each had about the resources around them and how each used those resources. The distinct cultural attitudes reflected their approach to life. The native peoples felt that the land was their Mother who nurtured them and who was to be revered; the settlers felt nature was a treasure box and whoever found the treasure—trees, waterpower, minerals—and was the strongest, was entitled to claim possession. Ownership was a large part of the settler's view. The Indians practiced consumption of the natural bounty as well, but it was often done with a reverence and with ceremonial awe.

There is no doubt that both groups impacted the land, but it would appear, from this distance of time, that the settlers' impact was more destructive to the natural pattern.

Here in this little ghost town are the remains of the emotions of many lives, mere flickers of their essence, resonating against the bluffs and the kilns, and through us. Here are the ghosts of ambition; the ghosts of reverence; the ghosts of high-spirited celebration; the ghosts of honest toil.

As you drive among the shades of those past lives, give a thought to where your values fit in amongst theirs. Can we learn something from their flickering essences? Do the dreams of the Indians, of power through cooperation with nature, speak to us? Do the hopes and plans of the settlers, who lived in the ghost hamlets, have messages for us? There were the men of business, dreaming of success; their wives and mothers, dreaming of stability and plenty; the children, dreaming of continual summer days in a rich forest that stretched for miles in every direction. Can we learn from them? All the dreams may live for a few moments in one's vision of what it was once like to live in the Big Woods. And the message may be quite simple: appreciate the beauty all around; so speak the flickering essences of the ghosts of years past.

Facts About Hurstville (11)

- South Fork Township, Section 12
- Lime kilns were built around 1872 by Alfred A. Hurst
- Lime kilns were restored by efforts of Jackson County Historical Society, the Conservation Board and other interested preservationists. Work began in 1982 and they were completed and dedicated in 1985. NHRP
- The Mesquakie, referred to as the Fox in early accounts, were present at the time of the Black Hawk Purchase in 1832.
- The newest town in Jackson County. P.O. established in 1897.

LOWELL

This town was platted in 1840, which was very early. The plat was an elegant affair, its vibrantly colored drawings show a well-designed city with broad streets and classical squares. But the plat was not a representation of the real village, only what such a place might become. It had been drawn to attract prospective investors from Back East with those possibilities. Often such plats represented what were called *paper towns*; they existed only on paper.

Lowell was more than just a paper town. It had a handful of houses and at least one mill, possibly two. The town was near the current dry bridge on the Hurstville Road which leads from Hurstville to Maquoketa. An archaeological survey conducted here in 1996 found fifteen feet of post settlement alluvium, or PSA, in the field where the town once stood. It means that since European settlers came into the region in the mid-1830s the river has deposited sediment to a depth of fifteen feet! This incredible tonnage of washed-in dirt occurred due to land-use practices, such as extensive farming, or changing the water courses. Think back on all the mills on this tour, and imagine the disturbance building a dam and a millrace would create.

At the base of this PSA (15 feet down) the archaeologists found the foundation of a mill and they surmised it to be a sawmill.

This site of Lowell, was once considered the richest land west of the Mississippi. It was well-watered, and it had a vigorous forest. Farmers in the early 1800s believed that the most fertile soil was where the trees grew. You just chopped down the trees, grubbed out the stumps and planted yourself a crop. They felt the prairie lands south of the river were a desert, and nothing would grow there since no trees were found on it. This whole region was known as the Forks of the Maquoketa, or the Big Woods. Early folks writing Back East referred to the little community of Springfield, or Goodenow's Corners, as "At the Forks of the Maquoketa", as well.

Lowell was an up-and-coming investment property, with its flashy plat map showing squares and broad avenues. The land was considered so valuable by it's developers that the lots were made very small, only 25 feet across the front. But alas, for the promoters, and early settlers, the fickle Maquoketa River changed course during a flood, and left the mills high and dry. The town dried up too.

Facts About Lowell (12)

- South Fork Township, Section 13
- The plat was drawn up by Samuel Munson, a good draftsman, who was also a partner with David Sears and Doolittle in the speculation of town lots.
- Thomas Wright had his woolen mill here for a few years before moving it to Maquoketa.
- At one time in the 1840s, it is said that a young entrepreneur was at work on a self-propelled wagon powered by steam. The entrepreneur's name was Ben Sears.
- Just to the east of Lowell's site, the North and South Forks of the Maquoketa River join. This occurs in a cornfield and it's not possible to see it from the road. Here is another spot that deserves a bench and a walking path. Our past calls to us from *The Forks*.

Our tour of The Ghost Hamlets of the Forks is ended. The businesses and most of the inhabitants of these little villages are gone. But if you have used your imagination, you may have conjured up their existence once more.

The hopes and dreams of their lives can come alive in your thoughts, and in a way, then, time will repeat itself, over and over again.

Ghost Hamlets—The Forks Driving Description

This drive has both hard-surfaced and gravel roads, and you may want to take that into consideration when picking the day for the drive. The gravel roads are well-traveled and except for a few weeks in the spring before the frost goes out, they are kept in good condition. Always remember to drive "to the conditions."

The lay of the land here in western Jackson County is quite different from that of the Mississippi River Valley. It is more rolling and open, but is nevertheless watered by many streams. The wild beauty of Eden Valley, and of the Maquoketa Caves State Park, is indicative of what this corner of Jackson County must have looked like in 1836 when the first settlers arrived. Use your imagination to see the land—the prairie, the timbers, the sandy-bottomed streams—as the first settlers of European heritage saw it then.

❖**From Maquoketa drive west on Highway 64 to Buckhorn.**
(1) On the way you will pass a sign on the right for Black Hawk Wildlife Area. It is about four miles west of Maquoketa, and is a good place to get out and walk around to see nature. On the highway again, you will soon come to Buckhorn, in its peaceful little valley.

❖**Just a little beyond Buckhorn on Highway 64 is Nashville.**
(2) Turn south on 100 Ave. to see this residential village.

❖**At the southernmost street in Nashville you are on 33rd St. Keep on this gravel road and continue west for about three miles and you will come to the site of Mill Rock.**
(3) It sits on the corner of 33 St. and 53 Ave. The school will be your destination just south on 53 Ave.

❖**After your time in Mill Rock is concluded get back on 33 St. for just a smidge and turn right on 50 Ave., or Y34.** This northerly route will cross Highway 64 and proceed through Baldwin, which does not qualify as a Ghost Hamlet, so no peeking! Stay on Y34 north out of town until 67 St. branches off to the west. At this intersection was the platted town of Franklin. **(4)**

❖**Keep driving north on Y34 until it meets E17.** The road passes the Royertown River Access along the South Fork of the Maquoketa River, and there are awesome bluffs to be seen. Eventually you will come to Emeline. **(5)**

❖**Our tour of Ghost Hamlets proceeds west on E17**, passing rugged limestone ledges and deep valleys. There are several county conservation parks along this way. They are: Ozark Wildlife Area, 45 Ave.; Pine Valley, 30 Ave., and Buzzard Ridge, E17. Locals used to claim that wild hogs roamed in the deep woods. Are they still to be found rooting about in the acorn mast? Its very doubtful, I'm told, but who knows.

❖**Just as the road is about to leave Jackson County and enter Jones County, and after crossing the South Fork bridge, we are in Canton. (6)**

❖**Backtrack, eastward, on E17 until 6 Ave. to the north. Make a left turn onto 6 Ave, and keeping right at 166 St., turn left again on 21 Ave. This road crosses the North Fork at the site of Ozark.** **(7)** I've been told there was once a covered bridge here, others say 'no'. Isn't history fun! The ghosts seem to be particularly abundant here for some reason. Do you feel their presence?

❖**Continue on 21 Ave. as it branches to the right and then heads north again. At 234 St. head east and come up to Y31, the Bernard Road.** You will come to a bridge that crosses the North Fork once more and here you are in Crabbtown. **(8)**

❖After Crabbtown we're "Back on the Road Again." Which reminds me, did you bring the Willie Nelson tapes? An absolute necessity. **Stay on Y31 to the south until E17, and the turn east, to your left, to Iron Hill. (9)** (Ask my husband, Chuck, about why we must bring the Willie Nelson tapes, he will be able to tell you. Something about never getting too much of a good thing.) **Drive on through Iron Hill to the east on E17 and you will soon cross the North Fork again. Turn south and exit Highway 61** to have a look at Fulton. **(10) (An alternative approach to Fulton would be on 182 Ave. off E17.)**

❖**Back on Highway 61, proceed south, and once again cross the North Fork.** Is anyone keeping count on the number of times we have crossed it on this drive? In the autumn and winter of 1996 an interesting Woodland Indian habitation site was unearthed on the western side of the highway south of the bridge. An archaeological survey was being made in preparation for construction of the expanded four-lane of 61. On the point of a narrow ridge, and about eight feet down, were found pottery shards, arrowheads and other projectile points, fireplace sites, or hearths, and some personal adornment ornaments. This site would have been inhabited at a time around 200 B.C. to 300 A.D., or around two thousand years ago!

❖**Turn off Highway 61 and onto Hurstville Road at the Kilns**. Hurstville **(11)** was once a booming town in every sense of the word. It had a lucrative business which was very prosperous, and it was a noisy place with the steamdrills and the blasting at the quarry.

❖**Stay on the Hurstville Road which now runs parallel to the North Fork**. The blunted point of the beautiful and wooded piece of territory between the forks comes to a head here. The exact spot where the rivers meet is hidden behind trees. They meet without fanfare and with little human observation. Near here several early settlers built a cabin only to wake one morning to find the river had risen overnight and was quickly filling their cabin with its icy water. They barely escaped with their lives. A few years later and up on a slight rise the town of Lowell **(12)** was platted.

Once you cross the South Fork Bridge and drive into Maquoketa this tour of Ghost Hamlets is over. Did you find the open door to the different time zones we have visited? Did you step through and live in another time for a few moments? If so, then you know the power of historical time traveling.

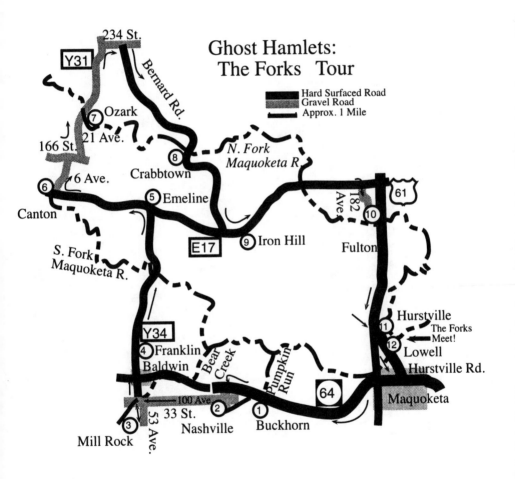

234 St.

Y31

Bernard Rd.

Ghost Hamlets:
The Forks Tour

Hard Surfaced Road
Gravel Road
Approx. 1 Mile

⑦ Ozark

21 Ave.

166 St.

⑧

*N. Fork
Maquoketa R.*

6 Ave.

Crabbtown

⑥

⑤ Emeline

182 Ave.

61

Canton

⑩

*S. Fork
Maquoketa R.*

E17

⑨ Iron Hill

Fulton

Hurstville

⑪   The Forks
       Meet!

Y34

⑫ Lowell

④ Franklin
Baldwin

Bear Creek

Pumpkin Run

Hurstville Rd.

64

Maquoketa

100 Ave.

② ①

53 Ave.

33 St.

③

Mill Rock

Nashville

Buckhorn

109

Chapter *7*

Ghost Hamlets II–
Old Stagecoach Road

"The happiest heart that ever beat
Was in some quiet breast
That found the common daylight sweet
And left to Heaven the rest."

John Vance Cheney

OLD STAGECOACH ROAD

The Forks Tour of Ghost Hamlets may have aroused your interest and sharpened your appetite for more long-gone little villages. If so, here is another tour, in another part of the county.

We might have called this tour the "Plum River Ghost Hamlets", named for the Plum River Fault that lies under the ridge where Highway 64 travels from Maquoketa to Preston and on to Sabula. It is an ancient fault line that has not been active for thousands of years but has influenced the county's topography nonetheless.

A stage coach road came to link the little villages; it went west from Sabula, to Sterling, Mount Algor, Van Buren, and on to Spragueville, Union Centre and then Maquoketa.

Old accounts tell of the very tall prairie grasses west of Sabula, so tall that a man riding a horse was covered over by them. Farther on to the west, at Copper Creek, the land was known to be so wild that it was said packs of wolves roamed at noon. Yet the area around Van Buren, or Buckeye, was settled by the time of the Bellevue War in 1839; several of the participants in "the war" were from Buckeye.

The towns of Preston and Miles were latecomers and really became viable when the railroad forsook the old stage route a few miles north and came through their communities.

So, for thirty-five to forty years, between settlement and the coming of the trains, the villages on the stage route met the needs of the pioneer settlers. All through the years—of travel by oxen, of log cabin homes, of the Civil War and its shortages and hardships, of the development of schools and local government—the little villages served their community with vigor. Their success, unlike the villages on the Maquoketa forks, didn't rely on water power. There were, however, a few mills along the Maquoketa River; Spragueville had several. What attracted the settlers to this part of the West?

The people, and their oxen for pulling the heavy wagons, crossed the Mississippi River on a ferry from Savannah, Illinois, to Sabula, Iowa. In the winter they could walk across on the ice of the frozen river.

112

The Maquoketa River Valley with its wetlands and heavy forested banks was to the north and the dry prairies were to the south and held little attraction to the early farmers, and so the settlers moved west in a wide corridor which had open oak savannas, small prairies with large and small streams, springs, and heavy timber here and there. Jackson County in the early 1830s has been described as like a park in the places where the prairie fires swept through. The stately oaks spread throughout the grassland and it must have seemed ideal farming land.

Soon the communities had a stage route linking them, bringing the mail, supplies, and new settlers. The towns grew and were prosperous because of the stage and because of the schools and churches which attracted new families.

What was village life like? Was it like this?

> "Bright mornings, noonday steeped in sunshine, and lingering twi-lights. . . mignonette sweetened the air, and hollyhocks and sunflow-ers and trailing morning glories vie with each other. Creaking wag-ons passed slowly by and disappeared on dusty roads. No one was in a hurry, and perhaps, no one worried over many things."
>
> *History of the People of Iowa*
> Cyrenus Cole

As you travel through the sites of the villages try to see the land as it might have appeared in 1840. Try to decide for yourself what would have been tallgrass prairie, upland prairie, oak savanna or the deep woods. It's certain that the valley of the Maquoketa was heavily forested. But the ridge where the stage traveled might well have been a gravelly, short grass prairie over limestone bedrock. Notice the type of soil; is it deep and black, or does it appear lighter brown and thinner with some sand or gravel? How would the soil have appeared when first broken by the plow?

Add up the facts, the observations, the dash of intuition, and the door to that other time region may be cracked just enough to quickly jam a toe in it, holding it open for a glimpse of the past's secrets. Remember, getting into that other dimen-sion is more important for our kind of time-traveling than being one hundred percent correct on the facts of the time.

Watch for the glimmer of the past shining through the door you have opened with your observations, facts, imagination and intuition. Trust those intuitions and enjoy the trip. After all, we can only experience one moment at a time; taking in the relevance of a year or a decade or a century is cerebral, but taking in a moment's experience is sensory, emotional, and spiritual.

If you're not in search of history and are not a history-phile, just enjoy the scenery, the ride, and the good company.

THE GHOST HAMLETS II

UNION CENTRE

Union Centre had a name; it had a cream station, a church and cemetery, a school, a blacksmith shop and a post office, but it didn't have a depot and so it faded away.

What is left of the hamlet forms a triangle along the highway and several gravel roads. In the center is a wooded hill that once had a park on the north side. On the west side of the triangle there was a fine avenue of maple trees leading to a farmstead. Until a few years ago, a weathered, abandoned house with empty window frames and nearly black clapboards stood at the end of the line of maples. Some said this was where the post office had been, in the front parlor of the little farm house. Now the house is but a memory to the few who noticed its sagging charm. The maple trees are dying, too; they must be very old.

As we grow older we all play the memory game of what it used to be like and what it is like now. As you read the following please keep in mind that the "Now" is 1910, and the "Then", is 1850.

NOW AND THEN

• **Now**, 1910, the people live on luxuries. **Then**, 1850, on necessities.

• **Now** they live on the choicest viands, fine flour, preserves, pies, pudding, pickles and canned fruit. **Then** they lived on hog hominy, venison, fish, samp, potatoes, pumpkins and wild plums.

• **Now** they ride in splendid carriages drawn by fancy horses. **Then** they rode in lumber wagons, drawn by oxen.

• **Now** they count their money in dollars, hundreds and thousands. **Then** they counted it by cents, picayunes and bits.

• **Now** the children attend school in school houses well-equipped and study reading, writing, arithmetic, spelling, English grammar, history, geography and Physiology and teachers get $18 to $45 per month. **Then** they attended the log hut and studied spelling, reading, writing and arithmetic, and the teachers got from $1.50 per week to $12 per month.

• **Now** the evening twilight is melodious with the sounds of organ and engine whistle. **Then** it was made hideous by the scream of the panther and the howl of the wolf.

• **Now** money is an equivalent for all dues and the acquisition of wealth is man's master passion. **Then** the currency was an exchange of commodities or labor, and there was such a desire to pay back in the kind received that Squire Reed married Wm. Conway "on tick"

114

and waited till Conway was elected Justice of the Peace and then Conway married Reed to his third wife to pay the debt, no interest being allowed on anything, except money.

• **Now** at the last election, there were 165 votes polled. **Then** at the first there were 7.

• **Then** the people were all on a level, and sympathy and kindness were extended to all. **Now** pride and vanity show their undignified heads, and caste is seen in all communities and assemblies.

Annals of Jackson County, 1908-1909

If we were to add a third comparison for "**Now**, 1990s" you can imagine the contrasts. As you ride along, talk about what you would suggest for the "**Now**, 1990s" addition to each. Does it seem that we haven't made much progress in some of the categories? Here are some categories I might include in a "Then and Now" memory game:

• **Then,** many were forced to quit school to help at home, or get a job. **Now,** almost everyone has as much schooling as they want.

• **Then,** many young mothers died in childbirth or from overwork. **Now,** few die giving birth and the "overwork" is more a matter of life-style choice. Leisure is often an attainable thing, even before retirement. There is the leisure to garden, read books, quilt for fun not warmth, exercise, take some classes, travel. This leisure is an expected way of life for almost everyone here in the Heartland.

• **Then,** men died old men at 55 years of age, gnarled and bent from years of hard physical work. **Now,** they retire at 65 and start a new career of volunteerism or part-time work/part-time travel. Their hardest physical activity may be a hobby like biking or jogging. Some retire from their second careers at about age 75 to have more time to travel or play golf.

• **Then,** the man was the head of the house, and no one forgot it. **Now,** there are many single-parent families headed by women. But there are also innumerable married couples who share responsibilities and consider themselves in equal partnership.

• **Then,** 1850, people dropped exhausted into bed at dusk. **Now,** they stay up for the Late, Late Show on television.

• **Then,** 1910, people sat on the front porch and watched the fireflies come out, waved to the folks strolling by on the sidewalk and breathed in the sweet scents of lemon lilies and climbing roses. **Now,** 1990s, people turn off the Cubs' game and sit on the deck to watch the fireflies come out, wave to the walkers and breathe in the sweet scent of the roses. Thank goodness some things don't change.

> ### FACTS ABOUT UNION CENTRE
> • Fairfield Township, Section 30
> • Post Office established in 1863

VAN BUREN

What was it like to live in a log cabin? We've seen reenactments on television, but here are several firsthand accounts to help us see with our imaginations.

"In 1844 we crossed the Mississippi into Charlestown, now Sabula, where we were met with two ox-teams and hauled to Deep Creek. The log-house, wooden door latch with buckstring strings, hickory splint broom, a big fireplace, two beds with curtains around them below and above, was a wonder to me. We went upstairs by a ladder. There were two beds, and the rafters were full of hickory pegs (in place of nails), and on these pegs hung carded rolls of wool and herbs of every kind - for there was no doctor there, candle molds, a spinning wheel, a gun, fishing tackle, etc. It had one window with six small lights of glass."

Annals of Jackson County, 1910-13
Mrs. Anna E. Wilson

The town of Van Buren was called Buckeye by the locals like Charles Wyckoff who wrote about growing up there in the 1850s. He, more than any other regional writer of the time, tells stories that bring the past very close. He has given us that glimpse into the past and it is our task to use the time-traveler's tools—"toe in the door", "observation", "facts", "imagination" and "intuition"—to catch it and hold open the door for a bigger picture.

This story took place on the R.B. Wyckoff holding around 1848-50. Upon building a kitchen, he made it 16' by 36' with a swing partition, so when he wanted to, he could turn it into a dance hall. The partition was swung up to the wall, and there was a dance floor of 16' by 36', which at that time was the most elaborate hall in the country.

"BUCKEYE CHRISTMAS"

As I look back to my boyhood days I can see that kind old mother with sleeves rolled up mixing the material for those famous mince pies which only mother can make, besides the gingerbread and fried cakes that tasted so good to me, and as I write it seems to me that although she has been dead fifty years I can hear her say,

116

"Now Charley, don't touch those pies or that gingerbread or those fried cakes, they are for Christmas. Well, now if you will be a good boy and split those dry rails so when father comes he can build a fire in the oven, I have 25 more pies ready to bake and I will give you a cake and a piece of the gingerbread."

The spoken of oven was built of brick, arched over on top and with an iron door. It was heated by filling with wood and when the wood had been burned down, the ashes and coals were brushed out clean and what was wanted to bake was put in. Mother could bake 25 fine pies at one heating. I have counted 200 mince pies on the pantry shelves alone at a time.

At the time I am writing about, the company did not wait until eight or nine o'clock to come but commenced coming in the afternoon, often as early as 3 o'clock. At 4 o'clock supper commenced and tables had to be set in the dance hall. As fast as people came they were served as it was expected that all would be through with supper and the hall cleared ready to commence dancing by 6 o'clock. Should any one be belated they had to eat supper in a small place.

After the hall was cleared the music was generally furnished by Robert Westbrook and John Scarborough, well known in the Sabula area, which furnished as guests, the Canfields, Schramlings, Bards, McElroys, Whites, Vials and others. Hauntown furnished the Hauns and Griswolds. Bellevue furnished Hood Davis and others. Andrew furnished the Butterworths, Palmers and Snyders; Deep Creek furnished the Farleys and Dickeys, besides our home Baldwins, Osburns, Swaneys, Prussias and Hatheways.

There was the old time candlestick that used to hang beside the wall to hold the candles made from deer's tallow, and hog's lard. There was no Standard Oil in those days, and none of your whirl-around-stand-up-and squeeze-them dances. It was quadrilles, money-musk and Virginia reels. It will be remembered by the early settlers that my father was quite a singer and would often entertain the company with a song. John Scarborough would tell the very amusing story. The mince pies, the gingerbread men and the cakes were set on the pantry shelves and everyone helped themselves through the night.

I don't remember of any trouble at any of those dances, nor of anyone having too much drink, although on a little stand was a decanter filled with Mr. Haun's best, free to all who wished it, but right here permit me to say at that time there was no such a place as a saloon. In every trading post either in the back room or cellar there was a keg on tap free to all, and further, most of the young people belonged to some kind of a temperance society, but promoters of temperance quit trying to persuade people to do right and concluded to compel them by law, and I am forced to believe the temperance people made a great mistake in trying to make people be temperate.

Those from Sabula and other distant points often stayed until after breakfast. If snow was on the ground they came in sleds, if not they came in wagons with a board across the box or flat down in the bottom, and often with ox teams.

But just one more thought as I am an old man whose sand is most run out. Go back with me sixty years ago to the old swinging bed and help me raise my head on a cold Christmas morning, out of those warm bed clothes made from the wool spun by those busy hands of mother, and behold the row of stockings knit by the same fingers, hanging along the mantel shelf of the old fireplace, and see those happy faces as we pile out of bed and eagerly take out the little tokens left us by the man that came down the chimney. And together let us thank God that our lot has been cast in a Christian land, and that when He calls we shall meet that good old mother in the happy land.

Annals of Jackson County, 1907
Charles Wyckoff

The richness of that story is something to savor, to roll around in the mind like a piece of toffee is savored on the tongue. There is so much imagery to contemplate. If you are wondering how a beehive oven is heated, here is the instruction or receipt from an old cookbook.

Some people consider it economical to heat Ovens with fagots, brush and light stuff. Hard wood heats it quicker and better. Take four foot wood split fine and pile it crisscross so as to nearly fill the oven and keep putting in. A Roaring fire for an hour or more is usually enough. The top and sides will at first be covered with black soot. See that it is all burned off. Rake the coals over the bottom of the oven and let them lie a minute. Then sweep it out clean. If you can hold your hand inside while you count Forty it is about right for flour bread. To count twenty is right for Rye and Indian.

If it is too hot, wet an old broom two or three times and turn it round near the top of the oven till it dries; this prevents pies and cakes from scorching on top. When you go into a new house, heat your oven two or three times to get it seasoned before you use it.

Bake the Brown bread first, then the flour bread and pies, then cake or puddings and last Custards. After everything else is out, put in a pan of apples. Next morning they will be deliciously baked. A pot of Beans can be baking back side, out of the way with the Rest.

Old Cookbook, 1805

The essence of good living is good eating and a snug house, and it is fascinating to conjure up the scenes of simple joys that might have taken place in those early log cabins.

118

FACTS ABOUT VAN BUREN

- Van Buren Township Section 15
- Post Office established 1854
- First called Copper Creek, then known as Buckeye
- A dozen families from Michigan settled here in 1830s
- Several general stores, blacksmith, hotel, marble cutter
- There was a plat that appears in 1893 Atlas and Plat Book
- A population of only 17 by 1890
- Charles Wyckoff, writer of "Buckeye Christmas", was the son of R. B. Wyckoff, early settler and county recorder from 1855 to 1860, a politician who represented Jackson County in the Democratic Convention about that time.
- Early accounts speak of a huge spring on the site of Van Buren. Is it still there, or has it been plowed over?
- Otto Schmidt was the post master in 1879 and operated a general store in Van Buren, [See *Cemeteries* for information on his huge gravestone in Van Buren Cemetery.]
- There are accounts of the attempts in the 1840s to lure land buyers to the Van Buren township area with tales of copper ore found near the stream. 'The creek's banks had been "salted" with copper ore but soon the scam was discovered and the land speculator who devised the scheme was, it is said, run out of the area on a rail. He left—shedding a few feathers—to return no more, leaving only the name of the stream, Copper Creek, to help us remember the whole unsavory affair.

SIDETRIP

"THE OLD STONE SCHOOLHOUSE" & MAPLE AVENUE

In the autumn this drive should prove a very pleasant diversion, and other times of the year it will have special qualities to offer. South from Van Buren about a mile is a stuccoed limestone school on the west side of the road, known as Henry School No. 2. It has been closed since 1946 when the scholars began going in to Preston School. There are maple trees standing beside the school. It is said that the original landowner joined up to fight in the Civil War and his wife and children went Back East for the war years. When they returned home, people had been cutting across their land to get to Buckeye, or Van Buren, so the farmer built a stone fence all around his land and planted maple trees alongside it. The stone from the fence has been taken away over the years for building foundations or for crushed lime for fields, but 65 of the maple trees remain in a long avenue on either side of the school. They are about 125 years old and some are in need of a tree surgeon's expertise, but they will make a fine sight in the fall; buttery yellow leaves tinged with pink against an intensely blue sky. On such a day this road will glow and sparkle with color. The trick will be to go on just the perfect day.

Let us imagine the school children of a hundred years ago walking down the dirt road on a brisk, sunny morning in early October; the teacher stands on the stoop and rings the handbell. Children, carrying in one hand a slate and books bound by a long strap, and in the other hand a dinner pail, swing along in groups of two or three. Families of children wait at the end of their lane for other students to come by. The older girls walk together and just a little ahead of the big boys; the littlest scamper in and out and round about these two groups and tease and run so hard they're all worn out by the time they get to the schoolhouse.

At morning recess the girls sit in the fallen leaves under a glowing yellow maple, the slanting sun on their shoulders and heads, and play dolls. Each girl has brought her favorite doll from home to play with at recess; some dolls were rag dolls made by an older sister or a grandma, some were chinahead beauties with leather shoes and real hair. All were loved and cared for with tenderness.

While the girls are absorbed with dolls, the boys are climbing the nearby trees and pelting the girls with bits of bark and twigs to get their attention. Some boys hang from the limbs, upside down, and wave both hands—just before falling into the big pile of leaves raked up under the tree. They get up quickly to see if the girls have been watching; the girls never encourage such silly behavior but they rarely miss much either.

The younger children play on the swings or run around in a game of tag.

When the recess bell rings and they come back into the schoolroom, their hair smells of woodsmoke from the school stove, and of sunshine and cold. Their cheeks are chapped and red, and some noses run. There is quite a bit of coughing and throat clearing before the room gets quiet and everyone settles down to work on their lessons.

Lesson time for the second graders might be to come up to the blackboard for spelling. Many eyes of first graders went to the board and learned early how to spell words like F R I E N D, and S C H O O L, and A P P L E.

The fourth grade would come up to the teacher's desk as the second graders sat down to write their spelling words ten times each on their small black slates. The lesson at teacher's desk was to recite the names of the states of the United States. A helpful song is chanted by the students, and everyone in the schoolroom keeps one ear open to check its progress. The older children listen to hear if the younger are saying the poem correctly, and the littlest learn it almost unconsciously as they work at their seat-work.

Learning seemed easy in a well-run school and was often fun. But some schools had bad reputations for rowdy students.

> A woman could keep better order in those days than a man, if she had the nerve to quell the big girls, for there was some little gallantry among the big boys, but a man teacher had to have his track well-sanded. We had one man teacher by the name of Ramsey, who seemed to lack the required amount of grit, had probably been brought up on buttermilk. The big boys would put him out of the schoolhouse and hold fort and he had to give up the school.
>
> *Annals of Jackson County*, 1905

This story might really be telling us about a frontier custom call "barring out the teacher." At Christmastime, the tradition demanded asking the teacher, "Sir, do you intend to treat the school?" The teacher by custom refused, and the students would prevent the teacher from entering the schoolhouse until the treats, usually peppermint sticks, were given to them all.

Many of us had parents or grandparents who went to country school. The folks who went to country school have stories to tell and to share with us. My grandparents were both country teachers in western Iowa, a township section away from one another. He was at Hardscrabble School and she was at Sorrel Top. They met at a county teacher's function, fell in love and got married. Then grandma had to give up her school because married women weren't offered contracts in those days.

Grandma was just sixteen years old when she started teaching country school.

school with so many different ages of students. The old lady she was boarding with had advice about this; she said to pick out the biggest boy and give him a good thrashing!

So on the first day of school Grandma had some trouble with the big boys and she called one up to her desk. She told him to go out and cut a willow switch and bring it in to her, she looked at another boy meaningfully while she said this, and gave the first big boy the idea that she was going to use it on his friend. He went out and cut a stout stick, thinking it would be great fun to see this little tiny teacher just 5'1" thrash his 6'1" friend. But when he got inside with his stick, he found out differently. Grandma proceeded to swat him about the shoulders and on his bottom. He ran around the room, and she chased him, hitting him a good lick every step! She was quick, if small, and he soon ran out of the school, and on down the road to home! The other children laughed with abandon at seeing this sight, they were happy to see that big boy get a lickin' for he was a bully and made them all miserable. He was 19 years old and should have graduated from eighth grade seven years before, but he came back to school just to lord it over everyone. The other boy, his friend, became the best helper Grandma ever had; he cut wood for her, brought it in and started the fire for her every winter's morning. He wasn't very bright, but he proved an asset to the school in his own way. Grandma said he grew up to be a fine man.

Such an incident—using a stick on a student—would today cause a lot of trouble with the state authorities and the school board. But in those days the teacher had to be self-sufficient and resourceful. The grown-ups in the community felt no threat from a little bit of a thing giving a bully the thrashing everyone knew he deserved. It was considered alright to whip the daylights out of a boy, but it was never OK to verbally belittle him, so Grandma's first day caused her no trouble with the parents. She felt that her reputation followed her to other schools because she never had trouble with big boys in those schools either.

As you look at Henry School on the "maple avenue", remember your family stories about country school, and share them with your companions or write them down to pass on to the next generation. This is how the past remains alive.

MOUNT ALGOR

It is said that Mount Algor was once a thriving place, with stores and a school and many houses. But it is also said that when Miles began to prosper because of the steam locomotive, the businesses and most of Mount Algor's people—and even the buildings—"picked up and moved" to Miles.

I have an image of this town, its houses and trees, barns and bushes, all of it, making up a large and rotund woman. Her voluminous, colored skirts are spread out on the brow of the hill overlooking the valleys all around. Her skirts are a patchwork of blooming orchards, gardens of black soil stitched with tender green rows of spring vegetables, lilac bushes near the outhouse paths and hollyhocks beside the bright red barns. The white of the clapboard houses is accented by the green of lawns and little pastures.

The woman, Mount Algor, often laughs; sometimes she cries. The sounds of singing and the sounds of bells ringing, sleigh bells and school bells, come from her.

She gazes down the road at Miles and wants to be part of its fellowship and liveliness; she comes to feel lonely here on her windswept hill. So, ever so slowly, she stands up, uprooting trees and bushes, pulling houses off their foundations, and ripping off the front stoops; with the buildings and all of the green things hanging on her skirts, she slowly waddles down the road. She is burdened by the weight of the stores, and houses, the little buildings: chicken coops and backhouses. She leaves a trail of broken window glass, broken furniture and broken dreams.

When she gets to Miles she shakes out her skirts and all the buildings scatter over the town to become part of new neighborhoods. Now the woman is thin, her skirts are limp and hang straight down around her, and she seems to waiver and begin to fade from sight and from memory. Mount Algor is no more.

FACTS ABOUT MT. ALGOR

- On the line of Van Buren and Iowa Townships. Section 24 of Van Buren, Section 19 of Iowa.
- A post office was established in 1855, discontinued in 1875
- It was around 1872 when the town moved to Miles.
- The bell from the school was tended by a local family for all the years after the town's move until the Jackson County Welcome Center near Sabula was built in 1989; the Mt. Algor school bell hangs in its belltower.

STERLING

The 19th century farmers and their families who lived near Sterling came to town on Saturday night to shop and socialize. The women and children went together to the general store while the men congregated at the blacksmith shop or the feed store.

Just about everything anybody needed could be bought at the general store. There were shoes for the whole family, denim overalls for the boys and yards of colored calico to be made into dresses for the girls. There were barrels of salt and sugar, weighed out and put in paper cones; seed potatoes and pickled herrings. Everything a family might need was there, and many things to tempt them, that they did not need.

Ma wanted a cast iron kitchen range, big and black, that would have a reservoir to heat washing water and would keep the kitchen warm. She had an account at the store and when she had traded enough eggs and butter to equal $6.50, she would get her stove. Her butter was the finest in the whole township, so folks said, and most of the family's store trading was due to that butter—it was the means to barter. Ma also did the laundry for several bachelors in town, which brought in a little money, actual coins, to be kept in the cracked sugar bowl at the back of the little cupboard.

Ma and Pa didn't have much cash, but with the butter and eggs and the few coins, they never had to go without. The storekeeper always added a sack of hard candy, horehound and peppermint drops, for the children.

As Spring was fast approaching, Ma had to think of the seeds she would need to plant the garden. She had saved some seeds from last year's plants, and some would have to be purchased. The family had just boiled down thirty quarts of maple syrup, and that, along with the tree-honey, would do for sweetening until late summer. Then she would have to barter for sugar to preserve plums and make grape jelly. Sugar and salt were two things they had to buy.

A pound of sugar to a pound of fruit is the rule for all preserves. The sugar should be melted over a fire moderate enough not to scorch it. When melted, it should be skimmed clean, and the fruit dropped to simmer till it is soft. Plums, and things of which the skin is liable to be broken, do better to be put in little jars, with their weight of sugar, and the jars set in a kettle of boiling water, till the fruit is done.

American Frugal Housewife, 1832, Child

Coffee was also an essential, although Ma did like a nice cup of horsemint tea in the afternoon.

Bergamot Tea
3-6 bergamot leaves (horsemint)
1 cup boiling water
Steep leaves in the boiling water for 4-6 minutes so that it infuses the delicate flavor of the plant. Strain and serve in a heated cup. Sweeten with a little sugar or honey if desired.

Ma had one dainty white china cup and saucer that came from her mother; she kept it on the mantle over the fireplace and used it only for her tea. It was one little indulgence she allowed herself.

She hoped the "mushroons" would be plentiful come May. Last year they had found a pillow-sack-full of the morels. They tasted good with most everything, but especially venison. Ma dried them and kept them in a tightly covered stone crock, taking out a half a cup to use now and again.

This is how Ma dried morels:

Cut the morels in half, remove the base of the stem, and wash carefully. Dry them with toweling and thread them on strings, hang up to dry in a warm kitchen or near the fire. When they are crisp, in a day or two, take them down and keep them in a sealed jar in a warm, dry place. When ready to use them, take them from the jar and blanch in boiling water for 3 to 4 minutes. They taste just like fresh ones and can be used as the same.

Every little bit of garden produce and wild food the family could harvest, with gun, fishing pole or basket, helped stretch out the trade goods. Ma was going to save up for a kerosene lamp next, so the children could read their school books in the evening and she could read her Bible. Pa was thinking about subscribing to the Sabula Gazette, he could barter a cord of firewood for a year's subscription; he would find pleasure in reading after supper, too. They planned to do without store-bought food as much as possible until the stove and lamp were theirs.

When the trading and the visiting were done, the family headed home to do chores and eat a light meal before bed. Come Sunday morning, they would be back in Sterling, to go to the Methodist Church. It was just at the south edge of town and the cemetery was behind it to the east; the white gravestones standing there as reminders of the passing away of people who had once lived in Sterling.

An Iowa author, Ruth Suckow, gives us her impression of a summer Sunday service.

The long stained-glass windows, which were often memorial windows, were open at the top and bottom—the janitor had opened them with his interesting but awkward long pole. We could see the rich green of the leafy trees outside in the fresh hot air; the growing fragrances of the Iowa summer filled the church and were interfused with the music. Then the music ended, the organ still holding a long chord of "Amen" as the congregation was again seated. The summer dresses rustled, the flowers quivered on the summer hats, there was a movement of palm-leaf fans picked up from the hymnbook holders.

Some Others and Myself, A Memoir
Ruth Suckow

The store, blacksmith shop, school and church were the life's blood of little places like Sterling. When trains came, and then the Model T, it was easy to get to larger towns for supplies and the little places became Ghost Hamlets, but for awhile they were good places to be.

126

Facts About Sterling

- Iowa Township, Sections 15, 16, 21 and 22
- Platted in 1851, Post Office established in 1853.
- The Methodists built a church in 1854. Another was built in 1872 and continued to serve the congregation until 1931. It was razed in 1962 and its 90 year old bell, which had come from England, was given to Faith Lutheran Church in Andover, Ia.
- There was a population of 200 in 1913.
- In 1855 the town was platted with twelve blocks; a hotel, two stores, two cooper shops, a carpenter and cabinet shop, wagon and shoe shop, saloons, a school and a Methodist church.

In the places where the little towns once flourished, we see the beautiful landscape and we imagine the details of their every day life; then we become aware of the thread that runs throughout the human experience. That thread is the appreciation of beauty, found here in a fine view; a little church steeple peeping over the trees; the thick oak leaves turning their burnt red color—not only shining overhead, but making a rich carpet for the ground; the bluff rising up, swathed with a shawl of woodbine and wild grape vines.

"There are words that can only be read, never spoken aloud." Whoever said that meant, I think, that we can appreciate and share through reading, the beauty we see, but for most of us it is nearly impossible to speak of that which moves us. It is a fleeting thing to grasp and capture the wonder we see, but some authors can do the near impossible—seek them out, read their works and search for the thread of sensibility that has run throughout the human condition here on this earth.

Ghost Hamlets II—Old Stage Coach Road
Driving Description

This drive follows the possible route of the old stagecoach road. It may be overlapped by today's highway and the gravel roads. In places the old roads have disappeared, as can be ascertained by studying the old plat maps. The stage road is illustrated on our map by a dotted gray line. Its placement is an educated guess.

The real fun of this drive is imagining the stagecoach, the stage's team of horses, the dusty road, the surrounding prairie, the oak trees, and the pioneer settlers' way of life. If you were a passenger on the coach in 1855, what would be your destination? Who would be waiting there for you? What kind of life would you be heading for? Imagine your dress, your hairstyle, your health; and imagine your future.

❖**Begin at Maquoketa and drive east on Highway 64.** Union Centre **(1)** has an alternate road around it which passes the maple trees and the old house site. The road is numbered 312 Avenue. Summerhill was the name of the stone school sitting on the ridge. An old cemetery is nearby. Just to the east, this ridge descends to more flat land. We wondered if the ridge once plunged down into a raging torrent of glacial meltwaters; or into the riverbed of the Mississippi in the far past?

❖**At the junction of 113, turn north, left, to Spragueville. At 45 St. turn east, right, and continue through town.** The Jackson County Recreation Trailhead is on the left. It is a hiking/biking trail following the old train tracks.

❖**Turn north onto 421 Ave. and then east onto 58 St.** At the junction of 458 Ave. is the town site of Van Buren **(2)**. It is very hard to believe that this spot was once home to a hotel, general store, blacksmith shop and dozens of houses.

❖**Turn south on 458 Ave.**, to your right, for the side trip to the Maple Avenue. You will cross 45 St. before reaching the trees and Henry School.

❖**Come back to 45 St. and turn left, and head east to Mt. Algor (3)**. Mt. Algor was at the junction of what is now Z40, a paved road, and 45 St. The ridge view is pleasant. The town of Miles is just a mile to the south.

128

❖**Continue east on 45 St. until it joins Highway 64** for a short mile.

❖**Turn left off Highway 64 and onto 525 Ave, heading north and then east on 50 St.** At the junction with 550 Ave. is the townsite of Sterling **(4).** Here you will see a number of houses and the lovely cemetery.

❖**Proceed on 550 Ave. in a southerly direction and join Highway 64** once more.

❖**Turn toward the east, a left turn,** and continue on to Sabula. *Or,* **make a right hand turn and go back to the west on Highway 64** to Maquoketa, through Miles and Preston.

Ghost Hamlets II:
Old Stagecoach Road

Hard Surfaced Road
Gravel Road
Possible Old Stage Route
Approx. 1 Mile

58 St.

Spragueville

45 St.

Union Centre

113

Maquoketa ≈2 miles

64

Summer Hill

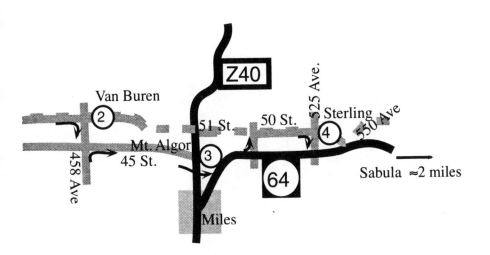

Chapter *8*
Cemeteries

> *Perhaps in this neglected spot is laid*
> *Some heart once pregnant with celestial fire:*
> *Hands that the rod of empire might have swayed,*
> *Or wak'd to ecstacy the living lyre.*
>
> Elegy Written in a Country Churchyard
> Thomas Gray, 1716-1771

Cemeteries are our culture's public gardens, where we display works of art, proclaim our ideals of beauty and truth, and maintain the stones and lawns with utmost care and reverence.

Autumn is a good season to spend time in graveyards. At the end of October is All Saint's Eve, an observance that for centuries has been the time when the spirits of the departed rose out of their graves and walked the earth. It was believed those times of seasonal change created edges, or doors, to another plane of existence. On that day, actual movement could occur from one plane of time to another overlapping or coexisting time layer. So those who died in the past would be alive yet in another dimension of time and it would be possible to see them on the last night of October on All Saint's Eve, also known as All Hallow's Eve in medieval times, and known to us as Halloween.

Today Halloween is a time for dressing up in costumes and going Trick or Treating. It is a time for celebration with candy and pranks—important aspects of the merry making. It is also a time to remember the people who have died in the past year.

Centuries ago the British Celts had an important festival called *Samhain* (Celtic: *End of Summer*) on October 31. They believed that the world of the gods was made visible to humankind at that time, and that the gods played tricks on their mortal worshippers; it was a time fraught with danger, charged with fear, and full of supernatural episodes. The Celts felt that without sacrifices and propitiations of every kind they would be unable to prevail over the perils of the season or counteract the activities of the deities.

The festival was also the eve of the new year in both Celtic and Anglo-Saxon times and was the occasion for one of the ancient fire festivals; huge bonfires were set on hilltops to frighten away evil spirits. The date was connected with the return of the herds from summer pasture, and laws and land tenures were renewed. The souls of the dead were supposed to revisit their homes on this day, and the autumnal festival acquired sinister significance. It was a time to placate the supernatural powers controlling the processes of nature.

Many authors have written of the elusive quality of time: H. G. Wells in *The Time Machine*; Jack Finney in *Time and Time Again*; Carlos Castaneda in *The Teachings of Don Juan*; Louis L'Amour in *The Lonesome Gods*, and Jan de Hartog in *The Centurion*. The movie, *Somewhere In Time*, starring a young Christopher Reeve, is about a man who falls in love with the portrait of a beautiful woman of the previous century and travels back in time to the 1880s through sheer willpower. The movie is set on Mackinaw Island, at the Grand Hotel—a building changed very little in one hundred years. *A Portrait of Jenny*, starring Jennifer Jones and Joseph Cotton, is a movie whose plot is based on the concept of overlapping layers of time.

Vesica Piscis is a visual image, or symbol, of two overlapping spheres, which represent the visible and the invisible worlds. It is a visual metaphor for those moments when worlds overlap or interpenetrate and life is touched with a depth and meaning beyond our common experience. Some say it is when Heaven and Earth meet, or when the invisible and the visible intersect.

In my church, Maquoketa UCC, our minister, Belva Duncan, has instituted a ritual of remembrance and memorial on All Saint's Day, the last Sunday in October. We perform a simple but meaningful ritual. Each family representative or friend of the person who has died in the last year comes forward and says the name of the person to be remembered, and then lights a candle in their memory. It is good to hear the names, and I believe it is good for the family or friend to say the name and commemorate their memory.

In England the graveyard is known as "God's Acre" and the implication is of the holiness of the place. We are indeed, then, surrounded by a "cloud of saints" when we are in a cemetery. We have a commonality of belief which may transcend death, and being in the place of those believers who have gone before is an opportunity for communion with them and that faith. Whether the worlds do overlap, whether the dead visit their old homes, or whether we only commune with them through our remembrance, the autumn seems an appropriate time for it. With the world going into a deep sleep, with all green and growing things resting under the deep snow, it seems we are confronted with death all around us. Death is a part of our world's plan of existence and we can choose to celebrate it as mysterious but also very sure and natural.

Cemetery Hill

The cemetery, in the loess hills of western Iowa, sits on a high rolling hill with the best view in town. Below the hill and to the east is the Mosquito Creek valley, with the curve of old Highway 64 and a large cattail wetland busy with red-winged blackbirds. To the south is the water tower and beyond it are the green trees and roofs of the streets of Neola. To the west are more rolling loess hills and a white, winding gravel road. All of these are visible from the cemetery, it is the highest hill around.

It is said that before the town was settled by Irish railroad workers and German farmers there was a large Indian village just to the northeast of this hill. Legend has it that the railroad paid the chief of the group of Potawatamie a hundred dollars in gold coins for the right of way. Soon the village was decimated by smallpox and, over the years, treasure hunters have searched for the buried sack of gold coins. They once dug up a hog lot near the village site. It seems a fitting irony that the treasure seekers had to work in the hog lot— seeking the last wealth of the dead village.

Growing up in Neola, I heard the old stories and I imagined an Indian coming to this high hill at sunset and singing a grieving chant into the blazing western sunset for a lost people.

My grandmother thought of the cemetery as something of a park. Catherine Anne Crossley Newland was the daughter of English immigrants and spoke with a hint of an English accent.

Although she gave the impression of English reserve, she shocked the neighbors by wearing Grandpa's old overalls to clean the outhouse back in the pre-World War I days when no self-respecting woman would be seen in men's pants. She responded that Mrs. Bloomer could wear them and so would she when it was practical. She was considered a little eccentric, I fear.

Looking back now I realize that picnicking in a cemetery is not routinely done, but when I was eight years old it didn't seem odd. When Grandma proposed a picnic, on a warm July day, and at the cemetery, I thought nothing of it. I was her youngest "close by" grandchild, and we spent a lot of time together and were soul mates; Grandma was widowed, and my best friend lived in the country.

We took a papersack lunch and a jar of lemonade and walked up that long hill which began at the foot of Grandma's sidewalk, to wind through town for about five blocks; then we got to the steep Cemetery Hill. Here, there was an old, cracked sidewalk leading to the gates of the graveyard a long block away. The sidewalk was shaded by mulberry trees and the fallen purple and red berries lay in windrows on the cracked and steep walk. Our hands were soon stained with purple juice as we picked and picked the berries from the low-hanging branches by the way. They were our delicate appetizer as we made our way up the long hill.

Once inside the high wrought iron gates we followed the driveway to the little grove of pine trees that had been planted around the tall iron cross. On the cross was a statue of Jesus, hanging as on the cross at Golgotha on Good Friday. At the foot of the cross knelt another statue, this of Mary, his mother. She was looking up at the hanging figure, her hands clasped under her chin and her head slightly to the side. Her face was depicted as full of sorrow. There were angels hovering, I seem to remember.

One might think this grouping made for a less than joyful spot for a picnic, but that isn't so. We sat on the cement steps of the platform in the warm sun, with the cool, hilltop breeze blowing through the scented pine branches, all the statues around us, and enjoyed our lunch. We ate hard-boiled eggs sprinkled with salt and pepper, green olives (Grandma's favorite), and bread and butter sandwiches. We shared swigs of refreshing, lukewarm lemonade.

Rested and replete, we walked among the graves and Grandma told me about the people buried there. She pointed to an old headstone, eroded so badly that it was hard to read the names under the lichen. She told me that here lay my great-grandmother and great-grandfather Newland. A few of Grandpa's cousins, and an uncle and aunt were nearby. Across the drive and back up the hill in the newer part of the cemetery was the grave of my grandfather. We always stopped at his grave for a long while; Grandma sometimes cried a little. She stood with her lips pressed together and her right arm tight across her waist, left hand up to her cheek, and looked down at the stone that said "William S. Newland, 1877-1949". Then she would raise her eyes to the horizon and gaze unseeing over the loess hills minute after minute. She was reliving time with Grandpa, times of shared joy and hardship. After a while she would breathe deeply and visibly shake herself back to 1953 and her little granddaughter.

It seemed to me that Grandpa had been dead for a long time. I remembered his open casket in the front room of their house the day of his funeral, but I was only four then and it all seemed so long ago. Now, I better understand that she was still working out her grief and loneliness there on the sloping hillside of the graveyard. There seemed a link between her sorrow and that of the other woman, the statue, who grieved perpetually at the foot of the cross.

When we started home, we walked with a determination, anxious to get back to our places in the busy world. We left the statues, the long-dead Potowatamies, and the graves of our loved ones to their long rest.

The memory of those picnics, the stillness, the warm pine-scented hilltop—once blooming prairie—which now overlooked the town and green fields, is gently satisfying. I'm glad we had our *eccentric* picnics on Cemetery Hill.

CEMETERIES OF JACKSON COUNTY

Mississippi Bluffs
From up above we look far down
And see the little villages.
And many a quaint and pretty town,
A red school house like Turkish fez—
Here Black Hawk pitched his deerskin tent
And guarded what he thought his land—

W. H. Klose

INDIAN BURIAL MOUNDS AT NELSON UNIT, BELLEVUE STATE PARK

The mounds which are on the edge of the bluffs overlooking the Mississippi River are a short walk to the east from the park road as it loops back south. Individuals were often buried in the conical mounds along the Mississippi Valley, that was over one thousand years ago. With them were buried shell beads, copper ear spools, carved stone pipes, tools and food in pottery vessels. Sometimes their bones, wrapped in a bundle of deerskin, were found in the mounds. Their bodies would have first been left on a scaffold, then the dry bones were gathered and buried with ceremony.

Whether these particular mounds were burial or were constructed as markers, there are many burial mounds in Jackson County and these mounds here in the park are the most accessible.

They are bigger than I envisioned, their height blocks the view of the river, and they are smooth. The earth must have been packed very hard to keep it from eroding through all the centuries of rain and runoff. Perhaps the builders put sod on the mounds immediately.

The mounds seemed to have been sacred to all Indians, even to those who came hundreds of years after there construction.

The place where Indian ancestors are buried is sacred, not just respected as white people respect their cemeteries; a holy place of the spirits of the dead. The comparison between a mound and the belly of a pregnant woman has often been made. The woman is the provider and protector of life, and the earth, the Mother Earth, is also the provider and protector. She takes back her children into her body when they die. They rest in her body in death, as once a baby rested and waited for birth in its mother's body.

All cultures have recognized the sanctity of a pregnant woman's womb, but not all make the connection to the sanctity of the earth, our Mother Earth. The Indians of the Americas did.

"And not even permitted to visit the graves of our forefathers, our relations and friends? This hardship is not known to the whites. With us it is a custom to visit the graves of our friends, and keep them in repair for many years. The mother will go alone to weep over the grave of her child! The brave, with pleasure, visits the grave of his father, after he has been successful in war, and repaints the post that shows where he lies! There is no place like that where the bones of our forefathers lie, to go to when in grief. Here the Great Spirit will take pity on us!"

Life of Black Hawk,
Black Hawk

STERLING CEMETERY

This cemetery is very well-kept, with hours of maintenance done to keep it looking so well-groomed. There are some big trees here, too, which add to its character.

It is a lovely place to stroll through and is a perfect example of a small, but immaculately maintained, Iowa cemetery.

The day we visited here with the Cemetery Commission, we learned about the white bronze gravemarkers. Today they are in mint condition, although at the time they were set in place in the late 1880s they were considered inferior to the white marble or limestone headstones. Those marble and lime stones are now so covered with lichen and so eroded, that many are illegible; some have broken when the ground subsided. The metal grave markers, however, are in super condition, looking like they were set in place last year, not last century. White bronze markers can be identified by their good condition. If it is possible to read an 1890 headstone it might be metal, and when rapped on—respectfully, of course—the tinny quality of sound will confirm it as metal. Those families who chose the white bronze markers chose well for longevity, even if they were choosing to be frugal at the time. Look for one dated 1886 near the Scotch pine in the southernmost part of the cemetery.

By the entrance gate is a marker for a veteran of the war of 1812; his name is Simmons. It is necessary to constantly remind ourselves of the longevity of our heritage. Here is one example; here is a man who was old enough to fight in that war, and then moved West to our county.

To find Sterling Cemetery, exit Highway 64 between Miles and Sabula at 550th Avenue. Turn to the north and proceed about a 1/4 mile to 50th Street. At this intersection in Section 22 of Iowa Township is the center of the town of Sterling. The road, 550th Ave. was once Sterling's North Street and turning east on 50th St., to the cemetery one travels on what was once Main Street.

> *Death*
> *Fearest the Shadow? Keep thy trust;*
> *Still the star-worlds roll.*
> *Fearest Death? Sayest "Dust to dust"?*
> *No; say "Soul to soul!"*
>
> John Vance Cheney

VAN BUREN OR BUCKEYE CEMETERY

The Van Buren Cemetery is not far from Sterling. The local people, call it "Buckeye Cemetery".

Here you will find the largest headstone in Jackson County. (That's unofficial!) Otto Schmidt's stone is over eight feet tall, is carved from a monolithic slab of granite, and was set in place in 1906. (One source said 1913.) There are many stories about this stone: it came from Germany, by ship, over the Atlantic; several wagons broke down getting it from Davenport; bridges had to be reinforced along the way, and teams of draft horses were changed every half mile. I have no idea if any of these statements is fact, although seeing the stone I can believe most of them. In any case, it is one impressive piece of rock!

Otto Schmidt, 1829-1905, had a general store in Van Buren from 1870 to his death. On his stone it says: *"A Man Whom All Men Honored"*.

To get to this nice graveyard take Highway 64 between Miles and Sabula and exit off it onto 45th Street, heading west. Turn north at the next road, 475th Avenue and proceed about 1/4 mile past the junction of 58th Street.

COTTONVILLE CEMETERY

Cottonville Cemetery, in Section 27 of Richland Township, is known as *The Arlington of Jackson County*, or *Little Arlington*, because of the number of Civil War Veterans' graves.

This cemetery is just to the west of the bygone hamlet of Cottonville at the junction of D61 and Y61. The cemetery sits on a ridge which gives unobstructed views to the north and west. There are only a few trees here, but there is an interesting flat stone set in the northwest corner of the cemetery. It is not a grave marker, but a plaque set as a U. S. Geological Bench Mark laid in 1961 and stating that the spot is 1005 Feet Elevation Above Sea Level.

A head stone placed for Levi E. Hunter, who died at Vicksburg, July 15, 1863, has this inscription:

> *Although he sleeps his memory doth live*
> *And cheering comforts to his mourners give*
> *He followed virtue as his truest guide*
> *Lived as a Christian, as a Christian died.*

Levi Hunter was 22 years, 9 months, and 20 days old when he died.

The town of Cottonville was a busy little burg on the stage road from Iowa City to Maquoketa to Dubuque. As early as 1844 Rev. William Salter, local Congregational circuit rider, mentions stopping at Cottonville for services. According to Salter, Deacon Samuel Cotton, founder of Cottonville, was a descendant of John Cotton, the first minister of Boston, Mass., and a Puritan. Samuel Cotton's grave is here: 1785-1866.

In 1893 there were still several stores, a blacksmith, the Union Church, and seven houses. But today there are only a few houses and the cemetery.

BUCKHORN OR WATERFORD CEMETERY

Buckhorn Cemetery, founded in 1850, is on a steep rise just off Highway 64, to the north of the highway. It overlooks the area that was once Buckhorn. Little Pumpkin Run Creek.

Mr. Burleson, the early tavernkeeper, is buried here. You'll find his red marble marker on the highest point of the graveyard. Here and there among the stones, where the mower can't go, are prairie grasses—big bluestem and sideoats grama. I like to think of the old pioneers being laid down under the prairie grass, even if there are only a few waving spears left. Their presence is a reminder of an early community coming to terms with a new land.

> It was there on that hill that history tells us the first American flag raised on Jackson County soil was unfurled to the breeze, July 4th, 1840, by Anson Wilson, who bought the cloth and Thomas Wright, Jr., who painted on the stars and stripes. The cemetery, which today is so densely populated by our pioneers and their descendants, was a part of the Fayette Mallard claim. His sister was the first person buried there.
>
> *Annals of Jackson County,* 1906

141

PENCE CEMETERY

Farther west on Highway 64 is another cemetery on a steep hill, Pence Cemetery. It contains the markers of the Solomon Pence family on the upper, east side. Solomon Pence and his brothers, Wallace and Gabriel, came into the country in 1834 to blaze the Buffalo to Dubuque trail and to mark any possible fords on the Maquoketa River. They stayed, and were among the earliest settlers. They were independent of Goodenow at the Forks, or the people at Bellevue. Solomon's cabin was directly south of the cemetery as you look out toward the creek bottom, about a quarter of a mile east of Bear Creek, and near the foot of a low hill.

> In later years in that old log house, he several times entertained U.S. Grant, then of Galena. In after years Grant went on to be Lieutenant General of the Federal Army during the Civil War, and later, twice President of the United States.
>
> *Annals of Jackson County,* 1906

A long row of similar gravestones, all with the Pence name leads us to wonder what caused the death of so many of Solomon's children; five died at, or near, age twenty, over a ten year period. Strange and tragic.

Another early settler was David Scott. He and his wife had 14 children; one died as early as 1838, and is buried here. Another, a 19 year old son, was killed in the Civil War in 1863.

By stopping a moment by these gravestones, reading the names and pondering how life was then, we honor the settlers, the past, and become, perhaps, a little more responsible for the future.

MT. HOPE CEMETERY

Mt. Hope Cemetery is in Maquoketa at the southeastern edge of town. It is the final resting place of many of the early settlers of the town: names like Goodenow, Shaw, and Allen. One of the most influential men of the county was reinterred here in 1906, nearly sixty years after he died.

This man was Colonel Thomas Cox, born in Kentucky in 1787, it is said, in or near Daniel Boone's fort. He was a veteran of the War of 1812, serving in a company of scouts against the Indians at Peoria Lakes in October of 1812. He also served in the Black Hawk War and was involved in the infamous Bellevue War, some seeing him as a hero in leading the posse against Brown, some seeing him as a rascal who caused the deaths of innocent men. He was an official surveyor in 1837 of the Black Hawk Purchase.

Cox built his cabin in that year at Richland, a townsite he named on the north bank of the Maquoketa River a mile or two downstream from Bridgeport.

142

The area had many springs, and there was a rocky ford across the Maquoketa near Richland used by the Davenport to Dubuque stage in those early years of the county. Cox lived at Richland for several years, but was often away at Burlington as Territorial Representative from Jackson County for four or five sessions, beginning in 1838. In 1839, he and another man were commissioned to survey the new capitol of Iowa, Iowa City.

According to Harvey Reid, a local newspaper man of the last century and his biographer, he was a hard drinker and died of liquor's effects in 1844. He was buried, with no marker, and under a hickory tree near his cabin at Richland.

A curious aspect of this story is that near this spot is a moraine left by a glacier eons ago. Here and there lie huge granite boulders in an area where we usually expect to see only limestone outcroppings. Remember this, it has something to do with Colonel Cox and Mt. Hope.

Sixty-one years after his death, the representatives of the Old Settlers' Association of Jackson County decided to exhume Thomas Cox's body and rebury it in a place of honor. They went to the hickory tree and made a trench and by luck, or chance, found the black walnut coffin of a tall man that they identified as Cox. In June, 1905, his remains were moved to Mt. Hope Cemetery and a memorial service was conducted there for the community and interested state officials.

Rev. William Salter, venerable minister of the early days, who had been a friend of Colonel Cox, having conducted the marriage ceremony of his daughter in 1844, and having been present to bury Col. Cox later that same year, was there to bestow a blessing on his old friend's new resting place. The following day a grave marker was lowered in place in the form of a large granite boulder, five feet tall and weighing over 14,000 pounds. This boulder came from the moraine near Cox's cabin. Later a bronze plaque was affixed in commemoration.

This remarkable monument is near the mausoleum, and just a little north and west.

ANDREW CEMETERY

Jackson County was the home of another noteworthy man who was reinterred in the early 20th Century: Ansel Briggs.

Briggs, who became the first governor of the new state of Iowa in 1846, was born in Vermont in 1806. He moved with his parents to Ohio around 1820 and remained there with his wife and children until 1836, when he came west and evidently settled in Davenport for several years before moving to the area that would become Andrew, Jackson County, Iowa.

He built a sawmill on Brush Creek in Section 14 of Perry Township and a log cabin nearby. This is near a site now known as Bluff Mill. He sold the sawmill before 1845.

He was involved in local politics and was the county sheriff for two years. As a businessman, he had a freight service, a stage line, owned a mercantile store, owned and sold Andrew town lots, owned farm land, was a promoter for the beginnings of the city of Florence, Nebraska, and was involved in such business deals as the formation of an insurance company, a bridge company and a railroad company.

His term of office as governor has been called "weak", but he was a Jeffersonian Democrat, and as such, believed it best to keep from manipulating the government as much as possible. He signed the bill to create SUI at Iowa City. He must have been a hardy individual, for, while governor, he lived in Andrew and rode a horse back and forth or *walked* to Iowa City, there being no decent roads on which to take a carriage or wagon.

After he ended his only term as governor he moved to the Council Bluffs/ Omaha region. Between the years 1856-1875, Briggs lived in either Council Bluffs or Andrew. His first wife had died in December, 1847, his second wife died in 1859. He lived at the Butterworth Tavern from 1869 to 1875 when he moved permanently to Omaha to live with his son, John S., and where he died in 1881. It is said by some that he died destitute, but there is little proof one way or the other.

In 1907, J. W. Ellis, secretary of the Jackson County Historical Society and a state legislator began a drive to remove the body of Ansel Briggs from the Omaha cemetery where he had been buried for twenty-six years, and bring him back to Andrew to be reburied with honors befitting the First Governor of Iowa. A monument was erected commemorating the man. The then governor of the State and many dignitaries and interested people were at the ceremony in the Andrew Cemetery in 1909.

From his monument, the view of the surrounding countryside is all about. He once had great expectations for Andrew and for Iowa. His work is now done, and ours goes on. We must continue to make this a good place to live, and a great place to visit.

HICKORY GROVE CEMETERY

Here, on a sloping hill, are the graves of two men who fought in our War of Independence, the Revolutionary War! Men who knew our country from its very birth.

Of the four known Revolutionary War veterans buried in Jackson County, half of the number are buried here. The others are: Lawrence Van Hook, buried at Andrew, and Eli Edwards, buried in Willison Cemetery, Farmers Creek Township.

Very little is known about these men or about their war years.

William Potter, who was born in Maryland or Virginia in 1767 and died in Jones County in 1853 was researched by the Daughters of the American Revolution, the DAR. They found records of a William Potter who served in Lieutenant Lamme's Company of foot soldiers, a unit of the Tenth Virginia Regiment. After the war he married Rachel Horner in 1792 and eventually moved to Licking County, Ohio. His simple grave marker was dedicated by the DAR in 1975. It is in the southeast lower corner of the cemetery.

William Sinkey was born in Pennsylvania in 1763 and was either a participant of the Cumberland County militia from April to June of 1782, one tour of duty; or a Flying Camp Ranger from 1776-1782, also from Cumberland County. He also died in Jones County, in the year 1849. His grave is near the front gate and to the north.

Both of these men came west to Jackson County as old men; probably with their younger sons or daughters. Perhaps they became friends, and sat by the fire, talking of Washington and Jefferson and the brand new country, The United States of America, which they had helped to create.

The Centenarian's Story

(At the battlesite, Washington Park, Brooklyn)

Give me your hand old Revolutionary,
The hill-top is nigh, but a few steps,
Aye, this is the ground,
My blind eyes even as I speak behold it re-peopled from graves,
The years recede, pavements and stately houses disappear,
Rude forts appear again, the old hoop'd guns are mounted,
I see the lines of rais'd earth stretching from river to bay.
Here we lay encamp'd, it was this time in summer also.

As I talk I remember all, I remember the Declaration,
It was read here, the whole army paraded, it was read to us here,
By his staff surrounded the General stood in the middle, he held up
    his unsheathed sword,
It glitter'd in the sun in full sight of the army.

Twas a bold act then—the English war-ships had just arrived,
We could watch down the lower bay where they lay at anchor,
And the transports swarming with soldiers.

A few days more and they landed, and then the battle.

Who do you think that was marching steadily sternly confronting
    death?
It was the brigade of the youngest men, two thousand strong.
Rais'd in Virginia and Maryland, and most of them known
    personally to the General.

Rank after rank falls, while over them silently droops the flag,
Baptized that day in many a young man's bloody wounds,
In death, defeat, and sisters', mothers' tears.

Walt Whitman,
Written in 1881

In Memoriam

It is good, I think, to visit a cemetery, for as one walks among the tombstones, treading the green grass and moving in and out of the shadows of trees, a peace descends upon the mind.

The dates on a tombstone read "1803-1885." My mind rushes backward in time, as if reeled in on a wheel of years, to 1803. I see a young woman holding a newborn baby, they are wrapped in a piecework quilt and the smell of birth is in the bedroom. The little house is in a hamlet in upstate New York, amidst the trees. Horses hooves can be heard on the dirt trail, and a bell rings through the quiet morning, its sound drifting up the valley. It calls the older children down to the schoolhouse.

I come back to the present and the graveyard, and as I walk along, I wonder about the people buried here; was Alonzo's life exciting? Did Nettie die in child-birth at 27 years of age? How did these three children die, so young and one year after the other? What games did they play? What songs did they sing? Did they have a favorite toy? When they died did someone grieve for them, or were they barely missed? Were they petted and cuddled, or were they worked to death?

Just when I am near the point of being overwhelmed by the questions, the peace descends upon my mind. I realize that all the stories are under the ground and it really doesn't matter what their lives were like. Happy or sad, warm and fed, or cold and hungry, they all lie in the arms of the Great Mother Earth, accepted and enfolded.

I feel that all the emotion of their lives has come to this—a quiet place on a sunny, Sunday afternoon. In a graveyard, it is always a peaceful Sunday afternoon. It is quiet and restful and worries dissolve. Yes, I know that my blunders, or if you prefer, my sins, may affect my children and their's thereafter may affect their children; the generations may be blemished by the sins done in another life, and the pain may live on generation after generation. The pain may remain alive in life— but, is *not alive* in death.

Here, in this place of graves, there is acceptance; it is a place of peace and generous love for all, sinner or saint. All are one in a graveyard. Nothing, not even death, can separate us from God's love. We may stray far from that love in our lives, but we are enfolded once again when we come to the peace of that perpetual Sunday afternoon.

Man's days are like the grass;
he blossoms like the flowers of the field:
A wind passes over them, and they cease to be,
And their place knows them no more.
But God's love never fails...

Psalms 103: 15-17

Walking among the grave markers, reading the dates and names and remembering is good, but walking among the stones and accepting what is coming to me, and to all human beings—to all life, is restful. There is a promise to be found here of acceptance and love.

The earth rejects not her own.

All that breathe will share thy destiny.
All these shall leave their mirth and their employments,
and shall come and make their bed with Thee.
As the long train of ages glides away, the sons of men—
The youth in life's green spring, and he who goes
In the full strength of years, matron and maid,
and the sweet babe, and the gray-headed man—
Shall one by one be gathered to thy side,
By Those, who in their turn shall follow them.

Thanatopsis
William Cullen Bryant (1794-1878)

149

For Mary, For Shirley

Mother, Mother, oh Mother of Mine
Where have you gone, Oh Mother of mine
I call out your name and you do not respond
I walk through brown fields, so lonely, abandoned
Through cornstalks and grasses now bent and forgotton

Child, Child, oh Child of Mine
I'm right here beside you, Oh Child of Mine
I hear your dear voice, and have not forgotten
You are not alone as you walk through the grasses
You're walking with me as each stalk snaps over backwards

Mother, Mother, Oh Mother of Mine
Have you gone into Night, Oh Mother of Mine
Can't you reach out your hand with all of your might
Won't you please come back over and rock me tonight
your child, so weary, so sad and so lonely

Child, Child, Oh Child of Mine
I'm here in the woods, Oh Child of Mine
I'm holding a branch like I once held your hand
There's a place you can sit, if too weary to stand
Beneath a great fir, It's Communion for kin

Mother, Mother, Oh Mother of Mine
Have you gone into Light, Oh Mother of Mine
Can't you please give a whisper and guide me today
Must I stay on this earth without your sweet smile
Must I carry my burdens without your strong shoulder

Child, Child, Oh Child of Mine
I've gone to the wind, Oh Child of Mine
If you listen, I'll sing in your ear everyday
my smile will touch you when with leaves it does play
And the clouds they will lift all your burdens away

Mother, Mother, Oh Mother of Mine
Are you now with our Savior, Oh Mother of mine
I've prayed that your memory will be with us always
I know that your goodness will be everlasting
I'm learning with God's help to have understanding

Child, Child, Oh Child of Mine
Honor my Spirit, give thanks to the Father
Honor my flesh, give thanks to the Mother
And give me the gift of just being Shirley
as you walk through the trees, the fields and the Glory

Charles Jorgensen

Chapter 9
Wildflowers

> *Spring seems to unfold her beauties slowly but she has*
> *something new each day for the faithful.*
>   Some Spring Days In Iowa,
>   Frederick Lazell

THE ADVENT OF SPRING

As Spring approaches, the crowns of trees come alive. A timber seen across flat and fallow fields, the late afternoon sun streaming it's level beams full-force, is like a Maxfield Parrish print: full of stylized detail, or a painting by Grant Wood, so real and yet so imaginary. Here a swath of poplars with their greenish-gray trunks and branches looking feathery on the ends, is juxtaposed against a rich green stand of cedars. The slippery elm are red-tipped, their bark is both craggy-rough and shiny, and they range in masses of wavy rows which seem to flow in and around the other trees like a torn-paper collage.

The stately oaks and shagbark hickories look down from the heights. Their branches lift free of the bluff, outlined on the bright sky, reaching for the pinky orange, sunset clouds floating overhead. Their shared colors are autumn brown and winter black; they are the forest cautious, waiting for "pretty, little May" to come along, before sending out their greenness.

A clump of staghorn sumac, the dried red combs pointing skyward, stands next to the blood-red twigs of the dogwood; their hues an enhancement of each other. Behind them are the black, thick, waists of the hickories; shaggy and aloof.

From this distance, the overall effect is one of softness. My hand longs to reach out and stroke the soft, plushy coat of the alive timber. Its fur would feel rough and springy, like the coat of a Husky puppy. The colors are harmonious, but separate, and it would be sensuously gratifying to ruffle and stroke them together: poplar and dogwood, cedar and sumac.

In spring, it seems possible.

AN EMBARRASSMENT OF RICHES

I realized last year, that this county has a rich inheritance in the spring. A family member who lives in southwest Iowa and is in her seventies longs to see wildflowers. She never was a hiker and knows of no place where wildflowers can be observed without strenuous walking.

The timbers she knew as a child, once carpeted with hepatica and Dutchman's breeches, are gone. She tells me that the large county park, near her hometown, is

154

kept mowed where once grew mayapple and sweet William. I realized then, how lucky we are here in Jackson County with our many bluffs of wildflowers.

Teilhard de Chardin, the mystic theologian, said that *seeing* is the whole essence of life. The wildflowers are there at our feet, but so often we do not see them. Instead, we see only the pasture that can support fifty cows; the black walnut trees that when cut and snaked out of the woods will bring big bucks; we *don't* see what is so near and can refresh our souls.

It is not just the exquisite and eye-pleasing form of the wildflowers that inspires, but also, their resilience. Wildflowers require no human hands to coddle, fertilize, and water them in order for them to do their jobs of offering nectar to insects. The insects will brush pollen on them and fertilize them for more flowers next year. That partnership of quiet wonder demands respect from all who can "see".

When you look at a bluff of wildflowers, you can capture just the barest hint of immortality.

> Consider the lilies of the field how they grow,
> They toil not, neither do they spin,
> And yet I say unto you even Solomon in all his
> glory was not arrayed like one of these.
> Matthew 7: 28-29, *The Bible*

SPRING'S SETBACK

Now, in the first full week of April, Spring has suffered a setback. No matter that the flowerbeds have been raked clean, the snowblowers run dry of gasoline and put up till next winter, no matter the crocuses are blooming and the lilac bush is a green blur in the icy wind; Winter has reclaimed the land.

The high pressure system in Canada which caused very strong winds and record lows to flood down the central plains of the Midwest, has crept over into the bluffland along the Mississippi.

The hermit thrush was seen near the back fence last week, scuffling along in the few leaves blown into the raked flowerbeds. She bobbed her reddish brown tail as she worked along, looking for insects. Now where has she gone?

The tulips, their green heads once held high in swelling bud, have all been laid flat. Their bed looks like a large animal had rolled in it!

In the country, the wise wildflowers are still hidden in the leaf mold. They bide their time, and their patience protects them.

This year was a year of exceptional weather. The devastating floods in Ohio and Tennessee and then Minnesota and North and South Dakota have been declared the result of global warming. On Easter weekend Boston had twenty-five inches of snow, and a week later, Iowa had as much as twenty-four inches. Such turmoil is scary.

I, however, believe the Earth is resilient, and, I believe in Spring. This is but a setback, and Spring will come again. Next year will be a perfect Spring, even if someone in the paper did say it should be added to the endangered list. If we all act in ways which allow the Earth to do her appointed tasks, Spring will be with us again; charming us with her soft breezes and her life, bursting all around.

> *In these vernal seasons of the year,*
> *when the air is clear and pleasant,*
> *it were an injury and a sullenness*
> *against nature not to go out and*
> *see her riches, and partake of her*
> *rejoicing with heaven and earth.*
>
> John Milton

SPRING DRIVES

How do you celebrate the spring? Do you have some ritual that welcomes the sun's warmth back to our region? Ritual has lost favor in this pragmatic age, but perhaps there is something you do every spring. I hope its not just oiling up the lawn mower. I hope it is more soul satisfying. Something special, like watching the sun rise on the Spring equinox. I pick five snowdrops from my yard and put them in a tiny green vase on my desk. Their exquisite blossoms remind me of the white stillness of pure snow, and the bursting, green life of Spring.

Some people rejoice in Spring by taking a wildflower walk, either on their own, or in an organized tour lead by a Conservationist. Many have favorite spots they visit each year, wildflower guidebook in hand.

For those times when walks aren't possible, I hope you will take a *Wildflower Drive*. As a part of your Spring ritual, remember, never pick wildflowers, their beauty is in their setting. Perhaps, some of you will have the resources to adopt an endangered patch of wildflowers, a special place you can visit and enjoy each spring. You may protect it as it pursues its Creator-appointed possibilities.

Spring is an unfolding gift, its days, with many new things appearing, make it *the season* of possibilities.

Joinerville

123 Avenue

This road was one of the *Great Roads* of Chapter 3. There are many early wildflowers forced into bloom by the morning sun's warmth on the rocks. They can be seen from the road that follows the bluffs before Pumpkin Run bridge.

We have been coming here for years and always find the sight of the bluff inspiring in its springtime dress. The white Dutchman's breeches and bloodroot frill the limestone ledges. They make me think of French schoolgirls of the last century. In uniforms of gray they walk two by two up the shallow steps leading to a massive cathedral. As they lift a knee to step up, the hems of their gray wool skirts, just above their ankles, lift and swing and white petticoats peep out. That glimpse of eyelet, scalloped and fully-gathered, is seen with each step. Here on this bluff, steps of gray ledges, I can see the frills of the white blossoms step higher and higher, from ledge to ledge. They sway a little, too, in the gentle breeze.

As the season continues, there are yellow bellwort, also called merrybells, dappling the leaf mold with hanging bells of gold. The white or palest pink blossoms of spring beauty take over the ledges and the ravines, and an observant eye can spot the preacher in the wood—Jack-in-the-pulpit.

The Little Prairie

109 Street

In early May the dry upland prairies are covered with the sky blue of bird's-foot violets. The color, from a distance, is mild and blends in with the shadows of rocks and grasses.

From the road the prairie here looks dun-colored, matted and seemingly lifeless. But close up, in this case, with the aid of binoculars, you can see the bird's-foot violets. Rock-cress is nearby with its tiny white blossoms on six inch stems, and the silvery pussy toes. One prairie grass is greening-up now—prairie dropseed. It looks like a ball of thin green blades; a very large, green hedgehog of grasses. In a month those spears will grow to a foot and a half long and be a cascading show.

There is one place, on the last uphill grade, the bridge crossed, headed south with the prairie on the left, where the prairie violets can be seen from the road. Feast your eyes. I hope the flowers are there next year and for many years to come.

Brush Creek Bluff
261 Avenue beyond the bridge

Beyond the iron bridge which crosses Brush Creek trout stream, is a bluff of tumbled limestone megaliths on the right and a deep valley on the left. On both sides of the road we spotted the upright, heart-shaped leaves of the wild ginger. It grows here in abundance, and very close to the ground. Its carmine red blossom, hidden under the upright leaves, is pollinated by ants and other crawling insects. The back of each ginger leaf is silvery with fine hairs which make it look like velvet tightly stretched over buckram. It has been a good year for wild ginger and it can be seen in countless numbers here. It looks exotic, like something from the design of a Persian carpet.

The late morning sun shines down on the steep bluff-face and touches the red stems of a family of petite ferns. They are just beginning to uncurl and are now luminous. They add another design, this from a red paisley shawl.

A room-sized, tilted block of limestone is completely upholstered in glowing, green moss. In tasteful groupings, grow the dwarfed flowers: hepatica, Dutchman's breeches, spring beauty and wild ginger. The lacy fronds of wood ferns in deep crevices soften it's contours.

On this road the blooms grow close to the roadside, showing off their charms in close-up detail.

This is a road to be visited often through the blooming season, to watch the progression of wildflowers; spring, summer and fall.

Green Island Road
500 Avenue

Along the first bit of 500 Avenue there is a high grassy bank where new ferns unfold and plum thickets set buds.

Then, comes the overlook, with its river and bottomland seen through the trees. It beckons to us, to stop and look, and look some more, filling our eyes with the sweep of the landscape and the richness of many shades of colors.

The 'B' level section of this drive is a special wildflower road. There aren't masses of flowers this year, but the foliage of Dutchman's breeches and hepatica covers much of the western slope. The right hand bluff, to the east, has scattered communities of wild ginger and spring beauty. It is the summit of this bluff that holds the jewel, for there, we catch a glimpse of the deep amethyst pink of the shooting star. It is a wildflower generally associated with the prairie, but here is the species called "jeweled shooting star". It prefers the damp, thin limestone soil on the bluffs of the Mississippi River. It is smaller and has brighter colored flowers than its prairie cousin.

The blossoms dance in the breeze of the bluff's rim. They are so intensely rose-crimson that they look more like cyclamens and suited to a greenhouse than the wildflowers living in harsh conditions on this windswept ridge. How extraordinary!

(After coming out of the timber into Green Island, proceed on Highway 52 to the north. Begin watching on the western bluff for false rue anemone. The bluffs are adrift in their delicate white blooms, and occasionally the taller shafts of the feathery Dutchman's breeches punctuate the field of blossoms.)

Maquoketa Caves
Off Caves Road 428

The Maquoketa Caves State Park is an outstanding natural wonder, worthy of many visits. It is not a place to drive through to see wildflowers, however, but the leisurely walk described here will unfold its impressive variety of wildflowers.

North of the entrance road and to the northwest of the Natural Bridge is the valley we want to explore. Wooden stairs and walkways have been built along the mossy bluffs. The numbered caves, which can be explored, lead off from the walkways. The valley is gentle and the runoff stream is only rarely active. The bottomland, now in late April, is carpeted with false rue anemone, its white blossoms and little round-lobed leaves seem to glitter in the day's last beams of sunshine. Many triple-leafed trillium, "in a whorl of 3", stand higher above the anemones, waiting to bloom in the warmer days to come.

A rustling in the leaves, up the valley side, calls our attention to a plushy, brown woodchuck. Though aware of our presence it isn't very concerned. He (or she) stops to sit in front of an outcropping that look like a perfect porch. There, on the bluff, the rocks look like the ruins of a Roman villa. Like something left by the legions as they abandoned Britain in the 5th century to defend Rome from the invading hordes. The outcropping seems like an open atrium surrounded by

159

three walls, and an arched doorway leads into the woodchuck's den.

Suddenly the stillness is charged with the loud voices of three excessively muddy young men as they emerge from a cave they have been exploring. Their voices echo back and forth across the valley and the woodchuck disappears into the rocks.

Here and there, we spot a plant we seldom see: squirrel corn. Its single flower stalk appears more yellow than the white blossoms of its cousin, the Dutchman's breeches, growing in profusion all around it.

The cave explorers move on, running to the next cave, and quiet once more claims the little valley.

Here we are enfolded by the green of moss, of tree and flower foliage, and the angelic white of the countless blossoms.

The Fern Road
182nd Avenue

The Fern Road has one wildflower in abundance this year, the Dutchman's breeches.

These white flowers are growing in small clumps and single stalks everywhere, on both sides of the road.

Its fernlike, delicate foliage covers the leafmold.

The twilight glows with white blossoms.

The placement of the flowers strikes us as rare—the Hand that planted them has devoted great care to their regular spacing, each having a bit of green all around it before the next white flower. They seem to have been planted in ordered arrangement over the rocks and hillside, but they bloom with abandon.

FINAL THOUGHTS

Writing this book has been like being on a long and leisurely vacation – the kind of vacation one dreams of taking in Provence, France. A dream of traveling the back roads from village to village, eating at the places frequented by the locals and really getting a "sense of place". True, while on my book-writing vacation, I've also gone grocery shopping, done a *ton* of laundry, shown up at committee meetings, visited with friends, relatives, doctors, dentists and pastors, directed the church choir and answered thousands of phone calls— and a hundred or so were even for me!

It hasn't been the kind of vacation where one gets away from it all. It has, however, been a vacation in the sense of getting to know an area well, discovering new places and coming home each day enchanted with some special, remembered beauty. An added plus was that I got to sleep in my own bed every night and I didn't have to get on one jet. The cost was also very reasonable.

We have been to England twice; once on an arranged tour with a train daytrip to the Cotswolds, and once on our own, renting a car and traveling all over Kent and the Cotswolds. We have also been to California (lived in Oakland and Daly City, just south of San Francisco for three and a half years), Wyoming, Santa Fe, New Mexico, the Black Hills of South Dakota and more. In the East, we've visited New York state, Vermont, New Hampshire, Maine, Massachusets and Connecticut. Our family has taken numerous weekend trips to closer destinations such as Omaha, St, Louis, southern Wisconsin and southeast Iowa to hunt for geodes. After each trip we came home with special memories: great views, good food, a quirky motel or bed and breakfast, characters we met along the way, and little towns and houses that said, "Aren't I appealing?". In England we visited cathedrals and public gardens, and did the same in Sante Fe. We saw wonderful scenery on all our visits.

It was my aim to do the same sort of thing here in Jackson County. We don't have many cathedrals, in fact, not one. I knew, however, we had scenery of great beauty which rivals that of many more fashionable vacation spots. It seems to me that Jackson County is as beautiful as the Cotswolds, or the countryside of New England.

Every drive can be an adventure, with beautiful scenery and new wonders. In June, watch for the state flower, the pink wild rose, in ditches or grassy verges. One might also see baby bunnies scurrying along the shoulder, turkeys running in uneven gait across a field of new corn, a bright blue indigo bunting flying into a plum thicket, or a hog-nose snake going down a gopher hole in a tiny remnant of a gravelly prairie. Smell the air, heavy with the perfume of new-cut hay and all the lush green growth of a wet summer solstice. Look overhead and see a light-show of pinks and purples piercing the sunset clouds with shafts of brilliance. Watch the full moon rise over the eastern hills and the mists drift over the river.

This adventure is not rare. The "adventure" described above happened on one, half-hour drive, within five miles of home.

In the writing of this book there have been many rewarding and special moments. I am thankful for the many adventures and the beauty. I hope that you, too, will feel a sense of place, find a special spot to remember with fondness and get to know more about "Simply Beautiful Jackson County".

GLOSSARY

Algific slope
Cold air slopes which receive cool air throughout the summer, transmitted from underlying bedrock, through crevices and sinkholes. Rare.

Biome
A major ecological community type, as grassland or desert.

Continental Divide
The crest of the Rocky Mountains, dividing rainfall and snowmelt into waters flowing to the Atlantic Ocean from those flowing to the Pacific Ocean.

Dogwood
Pagoda, or grey. An understory tree with greenish white tiny blossoms and purple berries. Found in timbers. Red Osier, found in wetter areas. Very red twigs in late winter. Locals know it as pigeonberry.

Gable roof
The vertical triangle portion of the end of the building from level of cornice or eaves to the ridge of the roof.

Grist mill
A mill for grinding grain; the grain is brought in for grinding and carried away as meal.

"Hausspruch"
Datestone on a building, often with year and inscription carved in stone. Popular in the early half of the 19th century.

Hip roof
The external angle formed by the meeting of two sloping sides of a roof.

Iowa Band
The group of eleven young Congregational ministers who came to Iowa territory as missionaries. In coming west in 1843 they vowed "each to found a church, and collectively to found a college". Their influence on education is considered to be an important factor in Iowa's high standard of educational excellence. The college they founded, Iowa College, has since become Grinnell College.

163

Jerkin head roof
Two sloped angels meeting a vertical angle coming down past eave line on wide side of building. Luxembourgian architecture.

Lime
Burned limestone. Used to make porcelain, glass, alkalides, in sugar purification, in treating soils; as insecticide. Process called slaking involves adding water to lime. Slaked lime is used in mortar, plaster and whitewash.

Loess soil
A very fine, loamy soil blown in place by the winds thousands of year ago during periods of interglacial dryness. Found all over Iowa, but piled very deep in western Iowa along the Missouri River to create the Loess Hills.

Mesquakie
Name of the Indian tribe which was mistakenly named "Fox" by early French fur traders. The tribe aligned themselves with the Sauk for a time, but had broken ties with them because Sauk were too warring by the time of the Black Hawk War. They lived in large villages and also roamed all over eastern Iowa in small family groups hunting and living a nomadic life. Their descendants belong to the Indian tribe living in the Tama/Toledo region today.

NRHP
National Register of Historic Places

Oak savanna
The descendants of a forest community which covered much of the Midwest. They include oak trees and the related plants, such as gooseberry bushes and certain wildflowers, which could withstand the acidic shade of the oak trees. Often on the margin between dense forest of river bottom and tall grass prairie. They have survived because they thrive in rocky soil, unsuitable for cultivation. The cows pastured there today serve some of the same functions as the buffalo and the fires of presettlement days, they eliminate the undergrowth and invasive trees. Watch for oak trees of massive girth with horizontal branches. They like to be spaced so each is outside the neighbors dripline and surrounded by grassland.

Old growth forest
The original tree stand of a forest; never harvested or logged-out.

Plat
The drawn map of a townsite.

Quarter section
A quarter, or one-fourth, of a township section; 160 acres of land. Proceeds from the sale of that amount of land was for the support of schools in each township.

Rabbet
An interlocking joint, or join in woodworking.

RAGBRAI
"Register's Annual Great Bike Ride Across Iowa"

Rock shelters
Shallow caves under overhanging limestone ledges or bluffs. Usually south-facing. Used as places of habitation by hunter-gatherer family groups of native Americans. Around 2000 B.C. to 1000 A.D.

Samp
Coarse hominy; Native American word. Hominy is a hulled and cooked-down corn dish.

Sarsen stone
A type of very hard sandstone, used in building the megalithic stone circles at Stonehenge and Avebury in England.

Side lights
Long, narrow panes of glass on either side of an outside entrance door. Typical of houses of the late 18th century to the middle 19th century.

Stucco
The mortar slurry applied over the limestone blocks of buildings which hardens into a smooth coating.

Understory growth
The bushes and trees which grow in the shade of the larger trees' canopy.

Voyageur
A French-Canadian boatman or fur trapper.

Windemere gravel
Glacial gravel, of the late Wisconsin period, with iron ore content. It has a smooth black appearance.

ABOUT THE AUTHOR

Jeanne Jorgensen, and her husband, Chuck, have lived in Jackson County for 25 years. They are both teachers, singers and nature lovers. They have two daughters, Caytie and Meg. Caytie is married, and Meg is a junior at Luther College.

The author is a graduate of the University of Northern Iowa, has taught in public school music education programs for fourteen years, and has been the choir director at the Maquoketa United Church of Christ since 1972.

Jeanne's favorite pastime is reading. She has read and collected books all her life. She loves nearly any material about England. In the past several years she has read extensively, searching for what she calls "a unique voice of women in literature". Writing has grown out of that love of books. In 1993 she wrote *A History: The U.C.C., Maquoketa, Iowa,* which is a history of the United Church of Christ of Maquoketa, the Congregational and the Evangelical Reformed branches as well as the current denomination. The book won a National Recognition Award from the Congregational Christian Historical Society.

As a part of the research for her second book, *The Charm of the Road,* Jeanne and her husband drove on nearly all the roads of Jackson County and walked some of those that could not be driven. She read local and regional history, and talked with many kind people who gave her many interesting insights into Jackson County. The book was first written in pencil, in many notebooks. Then the manuscript came to life on the electric typewriter. Then her future son-in-law provided a summer's use of the computer and the writer joined the computer literate. She eagerly looks forward to her next project.

CREDITS

Some Others and Myself
Copyright © 1932, 1952 by Ruth Suckow
Reprinted by permission of Henry Holt and Company, Incorp.

The Land
Copyright © 1951 by Jacquetta Hawkes
Reprinted by permission Beacon Press (Published under the auspices of Unitarian Universalist Association of Congregations)

Country Chronicle
Copyright © 1974 by Gladys Taber
Reprinted by permission Brandt & Brandt Literary Agents, Inc.

Life of Black Hawk
Black Hawk
Reprinted by permission of State Historical Society of Iowa

Wildflowers of the Tallgrass Prairie
Copyright © 1989 by Sylvan T. Runkel and Dean M. Roosa
Reprinted by permission Iowa State University Press

The Man With the Iron Hand
Copyright © 1923 by John Carl Parish
Published by Houghton-Mifflin

History of the People of Iowa
Copyright © 1921 by Cyrenus Cole
Published by The Torch Press

Some Summer Days in Iowa
Copyright © 1909 by Frederick John Lazell
Published by The Torch Press

Some Spring Days in Iowa
Copyright © 1908 by Frederick John Lazell
Published by The Torch Press

A Farm Picture, The Prairie Grass Dividing, and *The Centenarian's Story*
from *Leaves of Grass*
Copyright © 1926 by Walt Whitman
Bantam Doubleday Dell Publishing Group, Inc.

Who Drives and *Death* from *Leaves of Gold*
By John Vance Cheney
Brownlow Publishing Co., Inc.

Study Nature from *Leaves of Gold*
By Kingsley Brownlow Publishing Co., Inc.

Maud Muller
By John Greeleaf Whittier
Published by Houghton-Mifflin

Thanatopsis from *One Hundred and One Famous Poems*
By William Cullen Bryant
Published by The Reilly and Lee Co.

Elegy Written In a Country Churchyard from *One Hundred and One Famous Poems*
By Thomas Gray
Published by the Reilly and Lee Co.

The House By the Side of the Road from *One Hundred and One Famous Poems*
By Sam Walter Foss
Published by The Reilly and Lee Co.

Mississippi Bluffs from *Iowa Centennial 1846-1946*
By W.H. Klose
Self-published

Other Sources:

Annals of Jackson County, Iowa
Jackson County Historical Society, 1905-1913

History of Jackson County, Iowa
Jackson County Historical Society, 1989

History of Jackson County, Iowa
Copyright © 1910 by James Whitcomb Ellis
Published by S.J. Clarke Publishing Co.

The History of Jackson County, Iowa
Copyright © 1879 by Western Historical Co.
Published by Western Historical Co.

Every effort has been made to establish copyright ownership and procure permission for the reprinting of public domain materials. If anyone has knowledge of said ownership please contact the Glenn Oaks Publishing Company, Box 672, Maquoketa, Iowa, 52060.

ORDER FORM

The Charm of the Road
Drives in Jackson County

Price information: Each book is $17.95

Discount order rates:

1-2	None
3-9	20%
10+	40%

To determine the cost of your order: ✍

1. Number of books x $17.95 =   _____

2. Your discount, if applicable, of _____ % = _____

    (see discount order rates above)

3. Subtotal (Subtract Line 2 from Line 1) =   _____

4. Sales Tax - Add 6% of Line 3, if this order is

    placed to an Iowa address =   _____

5. Add Shipping & Handling costs of $3.95/book _____

6. Add Lines 3, 4 & 5 for your total =   _____

Books will be shipped upon receipt of payment. Send check or money order to:

Glenn Oaks Publishing
P. O. Box 672
Maquoketa, IA 52060

Allow 5 to 10 days for delivery.

ORDER FORM

The Charm of the Road
Drives in Jackson County

Price information: Each book is $17.95

Discount order rates:

1-2	None
3-9	20%
10+	40%

To determine the cost of your order: ✍️

1. Number of books x $17.95 = _____

2. Your discount, if applicable, of _____ % = _____

   (see discount order rates above)

3. Subtotal (Subtract Line 2 from Line 1) = _____

4. Sales Tax - Add 6% of Line 3, if this order is

   placed to an Iowa address = _____

5. Add Shipping & Handling costs of $3.95/book _____

6. Add Lines 3, 4 & 5 for your total = _____

Books will be shipped upon receipt of payment. Send check or money order to:

Glenn Oaks Publishing
P. O. Box 672
Maquoketa, IA 52060

Allow 5 to 10 days for delivery.